10 EASY LESSONS

D0771556

SLAP BASS

by

Peter Gelling

For more information on the *10 Easy Lessons, Teach Yourself* series contact;
Charles Dumont & Son Inc.
1085 Dumont Drive
Voorhees, New Jersey 08043
Ph: (856) 346 3452
Fax: (856) 346 9100
www.dumontmusic.com

Contents

Introduction

The bass player, together with the drummer, form what is called the 'rhythm section' of a group. They create the backing beat, driving force and 'tightness' necessary for a successful group.

10 Easy Lessons for Slap Bass is suitable for beginners, but it would be preferable to have some knowledge of bass playing before starting this book. *10 Easy Lessons for Bass* is suggested as a primer. During the course of 10 Easy Lessons for Slap Bass, you will learn basic slapping and popping techniques as well as a variety of articulations and left hand techniques which will make your playing come alive and sound more professional. Along the way you will learn many exciting bass lines which make use of these techniques and cover all of the common note and rest values used in music, along with the scales, arpeggios and fingering patterns used by the world's best bass players. A variety of styles are covered including Heavy Rock, Pop Rock, Funk, Blues and R&B. There is also a lesson on how to work with a drummer. All the examples sound great and are fun to play. Anyone who completes this book will be well on the way to being an excellent Slap bass player.

The best and fastest way to learn is to use this book in conjunction with:

1.   Buying sheet music and song books of your favourite recording artists and learning to play their songs,
2.   Practicing and playing with other musicians. You will be surprised how good a basic drums/bass/guitar combination can sound even when playing easy music.
3.   Learning by listening to your favourite CDs and playing along with them.

Particularly in the early stages it is helpful to have the guidance of an experienced teacher. This will also help you keep to a schedule and obtain weekly goals. To ensure that you develop a good sense of time, it is essential to work with a metronome or drum machine every time you practice.

For more information on the *10 Easy Lessons, Learn to Play* series contact;
L.T.P Pty Ltd
email: info@learntoplaymusic.com.
or visit our website;
www.learntoplaymusic.com

Approach to Practice

From the beginning you should set yourself a goal. Many people learn bass because of a desire to play like their favourite artist (e.g. Bootsy Collins), or to play a certain style of music (e.g. Funk, Rock etc.). Motivations such as these will help you to persevere through the more difficult sections of work. As your playing develops it will be important to adjust and update your goals.

It is important to have a correct approach to practice. You will benefit more from several short practices (e.g. 30-60 minutes per day) than one or two long sessions per week. This is especially so in the early stages, because of the basic nature of the material being studied. In a practice session you should divide your time evenly between the study of new material and the revision of past work. It is a common mistake for semi-advanced students to practice only the pieces they can already play well. Although this is more enjoyable, it is not a very satisfactory method of practice. You should also try to correct mistakes and experiment with new ideas. It is the author's belief that an experienced teacher will be an invaluable aid to your progress.

Bass Guitars

Bass guitars have **pickups** (a type of inbuilt microphone) and need to be plugged into an **amplifier** (Amp) to be heard. There are two basic types of pickups, one being **passive** (found in traditional bass guitars such as the Fender Precision and the Fender Jazz) and the other being **active** (found in many more recent basses such as Music Man and Alembic). Active pickups are more powerful and require a battery which fits inside the body of the bass. Some players prefer the bright sound of active pickups for slap playing, while others prefer the traditional sound of passive pickups. Before buying a bass, try out both types in a music store and if possible, get a professional player to help demonstrate the sounds they make before choosing a particular instrument.

*Music Man Stingray Bass -
contains active pickups*

*Fender Jazz Bass -
contains passive pickups*

Amplifiers

There are two main types of amplifiers, which are shown below.

1. **Combo** – which has a combined amplifier and speaker cabinet.

2. **Stack** – which has a separate amplifier "head" and speaker box.

Strings

Different types of strings can be used to create different sounds and feels. Round wound strings are the most popular strings for slap bass playing. The gauge varies between light, medium and heavy. A standard medium gauge would probably be the best to start with e.g. G = 45, D = 60, A = 80, E = 105. The heavier or thicker the gauge the "bigger" the sound will be. The lighter the strings the easier and faster you can play. Always clean your strings with a cloth after playing as this will keep the sound brighter. To get an optimal sound, and if you can afford it, change your strings several times a year, especially before an important session or recording.

Using the Compact Disc

It is recommended that you have a copy of the accompanying compact disc that includes all the examples in this book. The book shows you where to put your fingers and what technique to use and the recording lets you hear how each example should sound. Practice the example slowly at first, gradually increasing the tempo. Once you are confident you can play the example, evenly without stopping the beat, try playing along with the recording. You will hear a drum beat at the beginning of each example, to lead you into the example and to help you keep time. To play along with the CD your bass guitar must be in tune with it. If you have tuned using an electronic tuner (see below) your bass will already be in tune with the CD. A small diagram of a compact disc with a number as shown below indicates a recorded example.

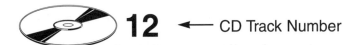 **12** ← CD Track Number

Electronic Tuner

The easiest and most accurate way to tune your bass is by using an **electronic tuner**.
An electronic tuner allows you to tune each string individually to the tuner, by indicating whether the notes are sharp (too high) or flat (too low). You can plug your bass directly into the tuner using the same lead that plugs into your amplifier. There are several types of guitar/bass guitar tuners but most are relatively inexpensive and simple to operate. Tuning using other methods is difficult for a beginning bass player and it takes many months to master. So we recommend you purchase an electronic tuner, particularly if you do not have a music teacher or a friend who can tune it for you.

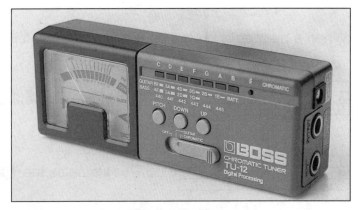

Electronic Tuner

Tuning Your Bass

Before you commence each lesson or practice session you will need to tune your bass. If your bass is out of tune everything you play will sound incorrect even though you are holding the correct notes. On the accompanying CD the **first four tracks** correspond to the **four strings of the bass**.

1.0 **4th String**
E Note (Thickest string)

1.1 **3rd String**
A Note

1.2 **2nd String**
D Note

1.3 **1st String**
G Note (Thinnest string)

How to Read Music

There are two methods used to write bass music. First is the **traditional music notation** method (using music notes ♩) and second is **Tablature**. Both are used in this book but you need only use one of these methods. Most people find Tablature easier to read, however, it is very worthwhile to learn to read traditional music notation as well. Nearly all sheet music you buy in a music store is written in traditional notation.

Tablature

Tablature is a method of indicating the position of notes on the fretboard. There are four "tab" lines, each representing one of the four strings of the bass.

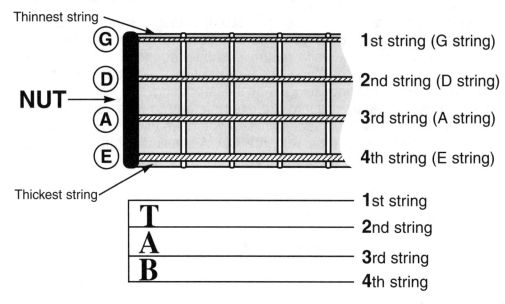

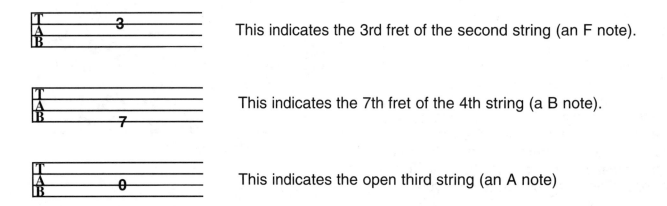

When a number is placed on one of the lines, it indicates the fret location of a note e.g.

This indicates the 3rd fret of the second string (an F note).

This indicates the 7th fret of the 4th string (a B note).

This indicates the open third string (an A note)

The tablature, as used in this book, does not indicate the time values of the notes, only their position on the fretboard. You can read the time values by following the count written beneath the tablature, e.g:

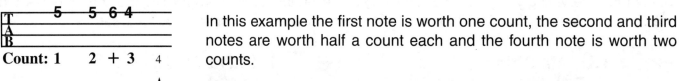

In this example the first note is worth one count, the second and third notes are worth half a count each and the fourth note is worth two counts.

The small number in the count is used to indicate where a note is being held or where a rest occurs.

Note: readers may need to refer to the tablature to determine the position of an example.

Music Notation

Music is written on a **staff** or **stave**, which consists of five parallel lines between which there are four spaces.

The Bass Clef

 This symbol is called a **bass clef**. There is a bass clef at the beginning of every line of bass music.

The Bass Staff

A staff with a bass clef written on it is called a **bass staff**.

BAR LINES are drawn across the staff, which divides the music into sections called **BARS** or **MEASURES**. A **DOUBLE BAR LINE** signifies either the end of the music, or the end of an important section of it.

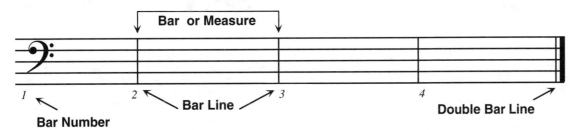

Music Notes

There are only seven letters used for notes in music. They are:

A B C D E F G

These notes are known as the **musical alphabet**.

Bass music notes are written in the spaces and on the lines of the bass staff.

The Quarter Note

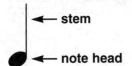 This music note is called a **quarter note**. A quarter note lasts for **one** beat.

Note and Rest Values

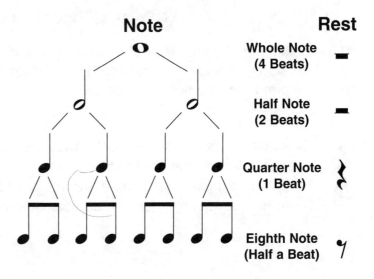

The lines and spaces on the staff are named as such:

Extra notes can be added by the use of short lines, called **ledger lines**, e.g.

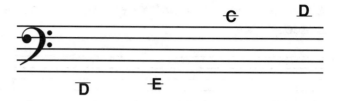

When a note is placed on the staff its head indicates its position, e.g.

This is a B note.

This is an E note.

When the note head is below the middle staff line the stem points upward and when the head is above the middle line the stem points downward. A note placed on the middle line (D) can have its stem pointing either up or down.

Notes on the Lines and Spaces

To remember the notes on the lines of the bass staff, say:
Good **B**oys **D**eserve **F**ruit **A**lways.

To remember the notes in the spaces of the bass staff, say:
All **C**ows **E**at **G**rass.

The Four Four Time Signature

At the beginning of each piece of music after the bass clef, is the **time signature**.
The time signature indicates the number of beats per bar (the top number) and the type of note receiving one beat (the bottom number).

These two numbers are called the **four four time signature**.
They are placed after the bass clef.
The $\frac{4}{4}$ time signature tells you there are four beats in each bar.
There are four quarter notes in one bar of music in $\frac{4}{4}$ time.

The four four
time signature

Playing Position

For a comfortable playing position, it is best to use a strap. A wide strap, approx. 2-3 inches (8-10cm) is best, so the weight of the bass is evenly distributed. Adjust the strap to a length that is comfortable. The full weight of the bass should be resting on the shoulder strap.

The bass should be angled slightly upwards (see photo), so that your left arm is free to move while you play.

Whether you prefer to sit or stand while you play, make sure that the position of your bass (strap length and angle) is the same so that your playing won't be affected.

Keep the bass close to your body so that it is easy to reach all parts of it when you play.

1. Standing Position

2. Sitting Position

Sitting Position:
Sit on a stool with a footrest to raise your right leg, or just cross your right leg over your left leg.

Lesson 1

Thumb Slapping Technique

The style of bass playing which involves slapping with the right thumb and popping with the right hand fingers is often just called **slap**. The best way to begin playing this style is to practice slapping the open strings with the knuckle joint on the side of the right thumb as demonstrated in example 2 and shown in the photographs below. The best place to strike the string is right at the end of the fretboard. This allows for a bit of "give" in the string and also forces the string down onto the frets, thus producing the sound. Make sure that you strike the string clearly and then let your thumb rebound up off the string like a drum stick rebounding off a drum. If you leave your thumb in contact with the string, it will deaden the sound and none of the notes will be clear. Notes slapped with the thumb are indicated by the letter **T** (meaning thumb) written above or below the note.

Quarter Note Rhythms

This is a **quarter note**. It lasts for **one** beat. There are **four** quarter notes in one bar of $\frac{4}{4}$ time.

Count: 1

 2.

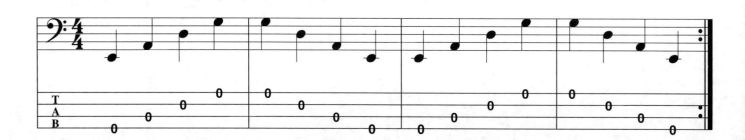

The Quarter Rest

Rests are used to indicate silence in music. There are different rests for different lengths of silence just as notes indicate different lengths of sound.

 This symbol is a **quarter rest**. It indicates **one beat of silence**. Do not play any note. Small counting numbers are placed under rests.

Count: 1

Left Hand Damping

As you strike each string with the thumb, be sure to damp the other strings with your left hand by laying your fingers lightly across the strings. In slap playing, damping out the sounds you don't want is as important as sounding the notes you do want. As you play all the examples in this lesson, listen carefully to your playing to make sure there are no unwanted notes ringing. If you do hear any, analyze which strings they are coming from and practice damping them out with your left hand. A good way to get used to left hand damping is to play a quarter note on the first and third beats of the bar and damp the string on the second and fourth beats (indicated by quarter rests) as shown in the example below.

 3.

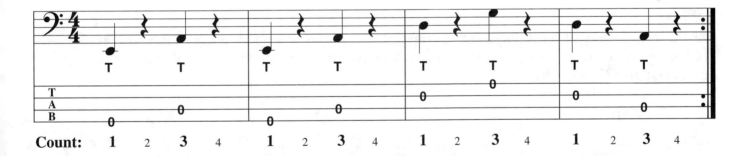

4.

Once you are comfortable with the previous example, try this one which alternates between strings on each beat, with no rests in between. This means your damping will have to be quicker.

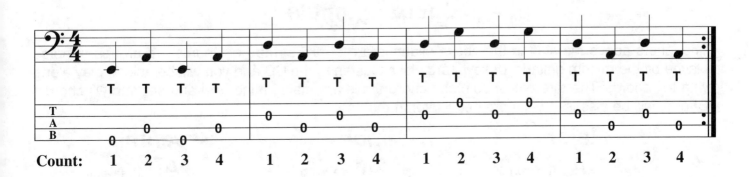

Using The Left Hand

The left hand fingers are numbered as such:

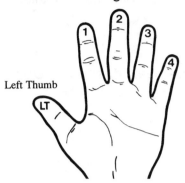

Left Thumb

The left hand finger number, if needed, is written next to the music note.

Left Hand Placement
Your fingers should be **ON THEIR TIPS** and placed just **BEHIND** the frets (not on top of them).

For greater support the left hand thumb should be placed behind the neck of the bass, approximately opposite your index and middle fingers as shown in the photo below.

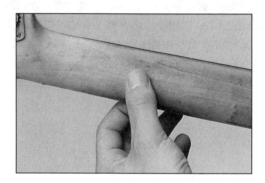

 5.

All the examples you have played so far have involved only the open strings. However, in all styles of bass playing you will frequently be required to use both open and fretted notes, often within the on bass line as shown here.

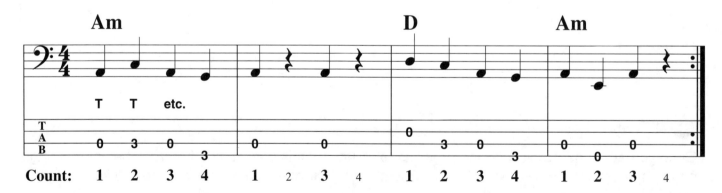

Chord Symbols

The letters above the staff in the above example are **chord symbols**. Chords are groups of notes played by the rhythm guitarist or keyboard player. Listen to the CD and you will be able to play along with the chords. The three most common chord types are major, minor (m) and seventh (7) chords. Chords will be discussed in more detail later in the book.

eg:

Major	**Minor**	**Seventh**
A (A major)	**Am** (A minor)	**A⁷** (A seventh)

The Half Note

This note is called a **half note**. It has a value of **two** beats.
There are **two** half notes in one bar of 4/4 time.

Count: 1 2

 6.

This example uses half notes along with quarter notes and quarter rests.

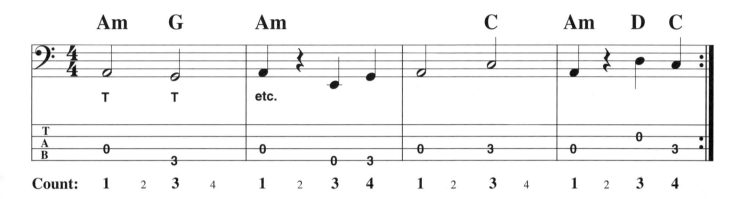

The Half Rest

This symbol is a **half rest**. It indicates **two beats of silence**.

Count: 1 2

7.

Once again, remember to tap your foot and count as you play regardless of whether you see notes or rests in the music.

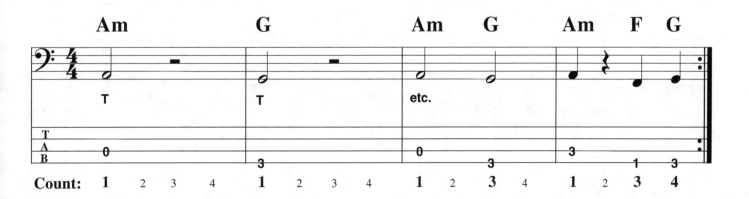

The Whole Note, The Whole Rest

o

Count: **1** 2 3 4

This is a **whole note**. It lasts for **four** beats.
There is **one** whole note in one bar of $\frac{4}{4}$ time.
The whole note is the longest note commonly used in music.

Whole Rest

Count: 1 2 3 4

The **whole rest** indicates **four beats or a whole bar of silence**. The symbol for the whole rest is very similar to that of the half rest. The difference is that the **half rest** sits **on top of the line**, while the **whole rest** hangs **below the line**.

 8.

This example uses both the whole note and the whole rest. Be sure to use the correct fingering as shown below the tablature. The stretch involved here may be difficult at first, but in time this kind of movement will become easy if you practice regularly. There is no **T** symbol here, but the notes are all slapped.

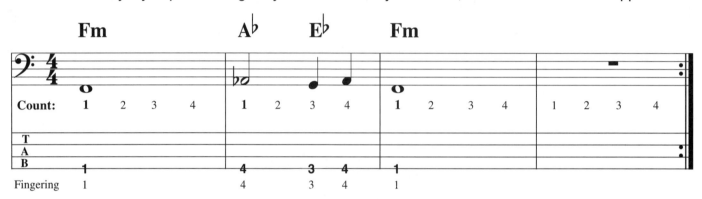

Left Hand Fingering

As a general rule:
1. Play notes on the **first fret** with the **first finger** of your left hand.
2. Play notes on the **second fret** with the **second finger** of your left hand.
3. Play notes on the **third fret** with the **third finger** of your left hand.

 9.

To finish this lesson, here is a left hand exercise which will help your fingers to stretch and also help them become more independent. Keep each finger down on the string until it is required to play a note on the next string up, e.g. when you play the A note at the first fret on the 3rd string, your second, third and fourth fingers should remain on the 4th string, only moving across to the 3rd string one at a time as they are required to play the notes at the second, third and fourth frets on that string.

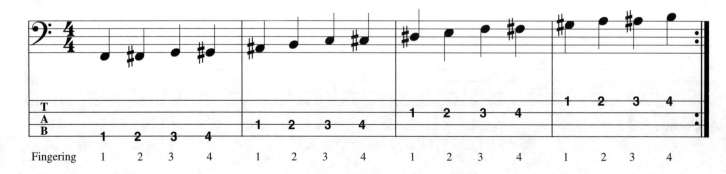

Lesson 2

Scales

A **major scale** is a group of eight notes that produces the familiar sound:

Do Re Mi Fa So La Ti Do

Here are the notes of the **C major scale**. The number underneath each note indicates its position in the scale. These numbers are called **scale degrees**. If you are not familiar with the major scale, see **10 Easy Lessons for Bass**.

C	D	E	F	G	A	B	C
1	2	3	4	5	6	7	8

The Blues Scale

There are many other types of scales which can be derived from the major scale by altering (flattening or sharpening) some of its notes and also by leaving out some of the notes. One of the most common scales used in Funk, Blues and Rock is the **Blues Scale**. Its degrees are **1**, ♭**3**, **4**, ♭**5**, ♮**5** and ♭**7** as shown below in the key of **C**. Notice how these degrees compare to the C major scale.

C Major Scale

C	D	E	F	G	A	B	C
1	2	3	4	5	6	7	8

C Blues Scale

C	E♭	F	G♭	G	B♭	C
1	♭3	4	♭5	5	♭7	8

 **10.**

This example demonstrates the sound of the Blues scale. You will probably recognise it right away, as it has been used as the basis of thousands of bass lines as well as lead guitar solos, vocal melodies and keyboard parts.

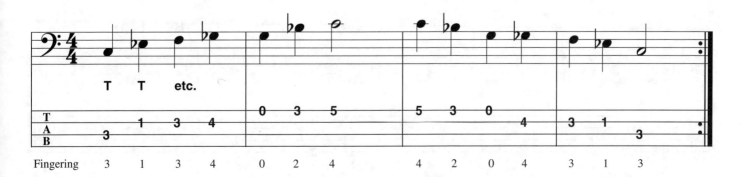

Moveable Fingering Patterns

There are many different fingerings which can be used to play the Blues scale on the bass. The most versatile fingerings are those which do not contain open strings and are therefore moveable, which means they can be shifted up or down the neck. The advantage of moveable patterns is that they enable you to play the scale (and bass lines derived from it) in all keys. One of the most common moveable fingering patterns for the Blues scale is shown below in the key of C.

Blues Scale Pattern 1

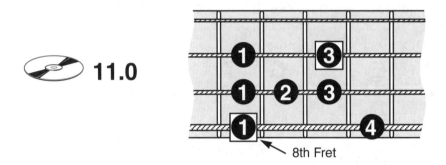

11.0

8th Fret

 11.1 Play this Blues scale pattern commencing on the **B♭** note on the 6th fret of the 4th string. You are now playing a **B flat Blues scale**.

Riffs

Written below is a riff style bass line created from the **G** Blues scale. A **riff** is a pattern of notes which repeats throughout a progression, but may be altered slightly to fit chord changes. Once you have learned the riff in this key, try transposing it (changing the key) to the keys of **F** and **A**. This can easily be done by locating the starting note and playing the whole line at the appropriate fret.

12.

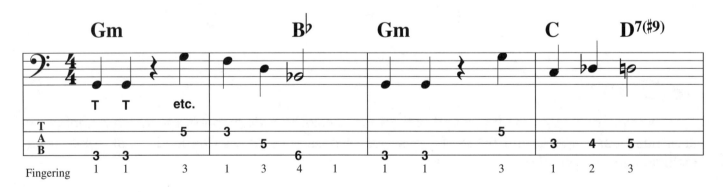

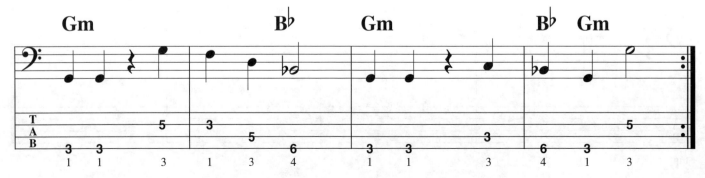

Blues Scale Pattern Variation

The Blues scale pattern you have just learned can also be played starting on the third string as shown below. The pattern looks the same but it begins on a different string. Like pattern 1, it can be transposed to any key by simply moving it up or down the neck. Here it is in the key of C.

 **13.**

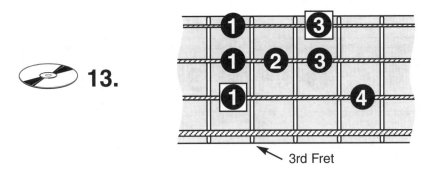

← 3rd Fret

The Dotted Half Note

Count: 1 2 3

A **dot** written after a note extends its value by **half**.
A dot after a half note means that you hold it for **three** beats.

 **14.**

The following example demonstrates a bass line derived from the fingering pattern shown above. It contains a dotted half note in bar 4. Pay particular attention to the fingering in bars 1 and 3. When two consecutive notes occur at the same fret on different strings, it is common to use the fourth finger for the higher note and the third finger for the lower note as shown here.

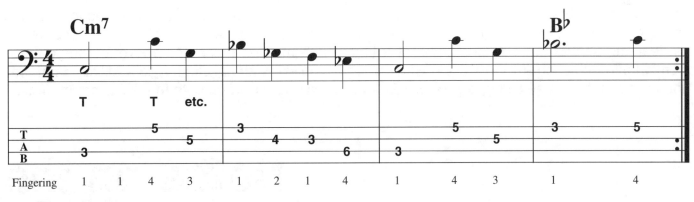

15.

Once you have memorized the previous bass line, try playing it in pattern 1 (8th position) as shown below.

Learning the Notes

To be a good musician, it is important to be able to play equally well in all keys. To do this you will need to know all the notes on the fretboard from memory. A good way to learn the notes is to take one string at a time. Call the notes which are not naturals sharps as you ascend and flats as you descend. A diagram of the second string is shown below as an example.

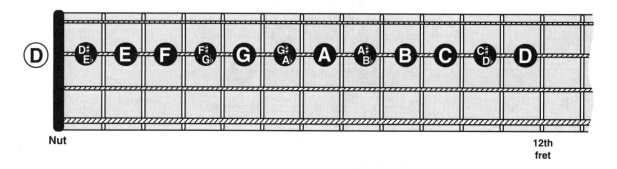

Nut   12th
                                                                                       fret

The dots on your bass are also good points of reference. You can use them to help the memorizing process. Play the notes at each of the dots and name them out loud as you play. The fingering is not important here, just the note names.

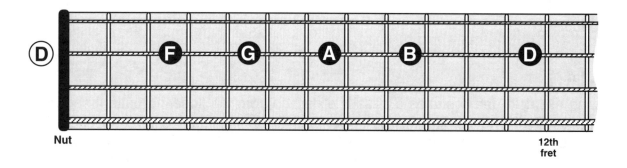

Nut   12th
                                                                                       fret

Next, pick the name of a note at random and find it as quickly as possible. When that becomes easy, move on to the next string. Written below is a diagram of all the notes available on the bass. Work on learning all the notes on one string at a time in the manner presented above. When you are comfortable with each string, try finding the same note on every string. Often a note will appear more than once on the same string, e.g. **B**♭ or **A**♯ on the 1st string occurs at both the 3rd and 15th frets.

Notes on the

Here is a Fretboard Diagram of all the notes on the bass. Play the notes on each string from 4th string is an E note and the note on the 12th fret of the 4th string is also an E note but is one octave higher.

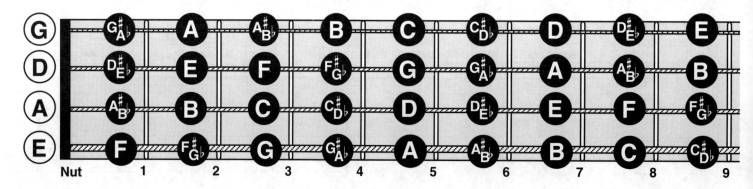

One more useful way of learning the notes is to go across each fret. Once again, use sharps as you go higher in pitch and flats as you go back down.

The Chromatic Scale

The notes **E F** and **BC** are always one semitone apart (one fret). All other notes are a tone apart (2 frets). Sharps (♯) and flats (♭) are found between the notes that are a tone apart.

$$C \quad \genfrac{}{}{0pt}{}{C\sharp}{D\flat} \quad D \quad \genfrac{}{}{0pt}{}{D\sharp}{E\flat} \quad E \; F \quad \genfrac{}{}{0pt}{}{F\sharp}{G\flat} \quad G \quad \genfrac{}{}{0pt}{}{G\sharp}{A\flat} \quad A \quad \genfrac{}{}{0pt}{}{A\sharp}{B\flat} \quad B \; C$$

This scale is called the chromatic scale and contains all the ♯'s and ♭'s possible. C sharp (C♯) has the same position on the fretboard as D flat (D♭). They are the same note but can have different names depending upon what key you are playing in. The same applies to D♯/E♭, F♯/G♭, G♯/A♭ A♯/B♭. These are called **enharmonic notes**. The diagram shown below includes all these sharps and flats.

Also notice that:
The 5th fret of the E string (A note) is the same note as the open A string.
The 5th fret of the A string (D note) is the same note as the open D string.
The 5th fret of the D string (G note) is the same note as the open G string.

These note positions are important to remember because they are the basis for tuning your bass to itself.

Bass Fretboard

the open note to the 12th fret. The note on the 12th fret is one octave higher than the open note, e.g. the open

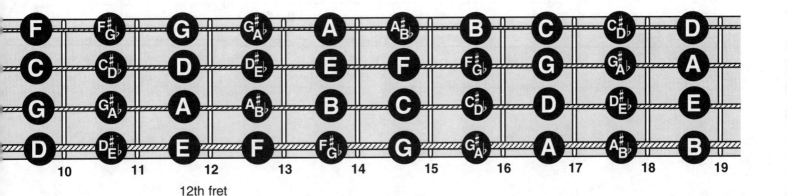

Lesson 3

The Eighth Note

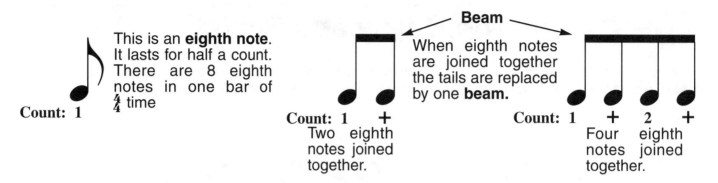

This is an **eighth note**. It lasts for half a count. There are 8 eighth notes in one bar of $\frac{4}{4}$ time

Count: 1

Beam

When eighth notes are joined together the tails are replaced by one **beam**.

Count: 1   +
Two eighth notes joined together.

Count: 1   +   2   +
Four eighth notes joined together.

Play the following example using the thumb slapping technique in exactly the same way as you would play quarter, half or whole notes. The only difference here is that the notes are closer together. Tap your foot on each beat and count out loud as you play. Listen carefully as you play and make sure all the notes are even in length, tone and volume.

 16. How to Count Eighth Notes

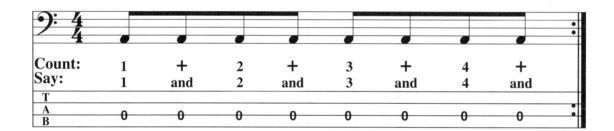

 **17.**

Once you can play eighth notes on the open A string, try moving across all of the strings as shown here. Once again, keep your notes even in length, tone and volume.

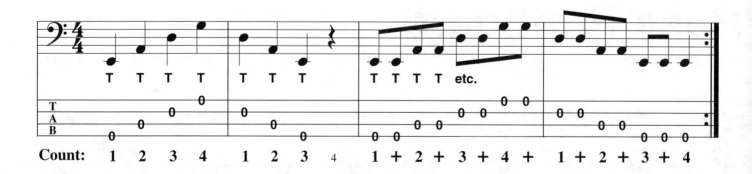

Here are some slap bass lines which make use of eighth notes. As with everything you play, be sure to use left hand damping to avoid extra unwanted sounds.

 **18.**

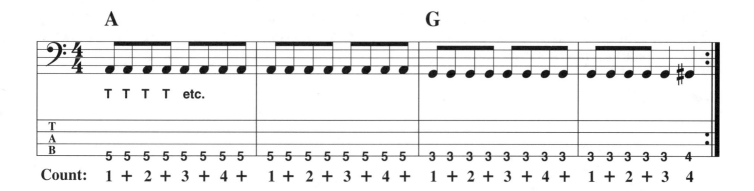

Practice your Blues scales using 8th notes as shown below. First run through the scale playing each note once, and then playing each note twice. Make sure all your notes sound strong and even.

 **19.**

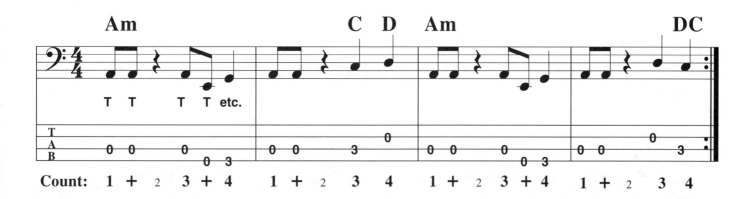

 **20.**

Extending Scale Patterns

As you learned in the previous lesson, it is possible to find higher and lower versions of the same notes in many different places on the fretboard, e.g. the note **G** on the 3rd fret of the 4th string and the **G** an octave higher on the 5th fret of the 2nd string. Because of this feature of the instrument, it is possible to repeat some of the notes of any scale within a fingering pattern. Shown below is the C Blues scale at the 3rd position with the notes G (5th) and B (flattened 7th) added on the 4th string. This demonstrates that you can start a scale pattern on **any** note of the scale instead of always having to start on the root note.

 **21.**

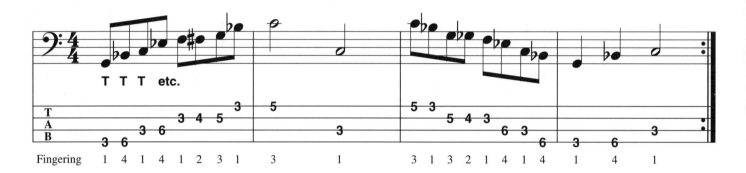

 **22.**

Here is a bass line which makes use of these extra notes. Once again, take care with the fingering of this example.

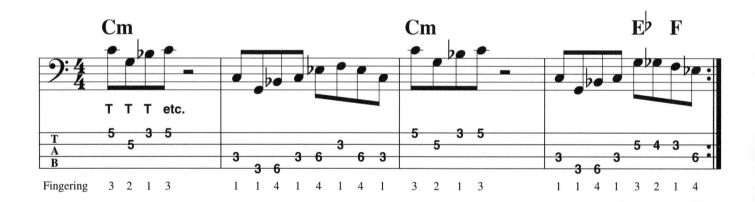

23.

This one is derived from the A Blues scale and makes use of open strings.

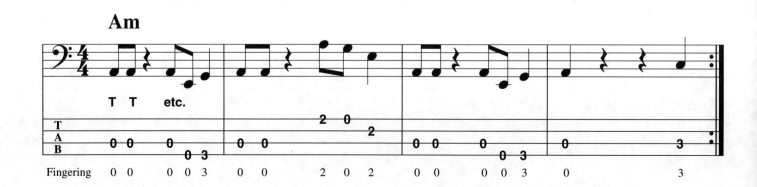

The Dotted Quarter Note

 A dot written after a quarter note means that you hold the note for **one and a half beats**.

Count **1** 2 +

A dotted quarter note is often followed by an eighth note.

 24.

Listen to the way the bass and the bass drum work together in this example.

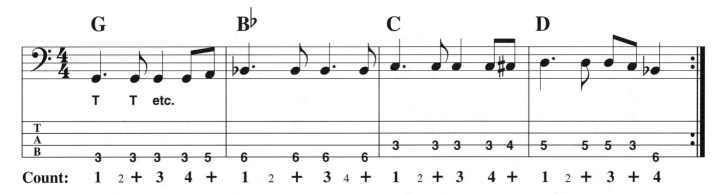

Syncopation

The example below contains another rhythm figure using dotted quarter notes. This time the eighth note is played first and the dotted quarter note is played off the beat. This creates an effect known as **syncopation**, which means displacing the normal flow of accents, usually from **on** the beat to **off** the beat. Practice it slowly at first and count carefully as you play, tapping your foot on each beat. It is important to practice all new rhythms with a metronome or drum machine until you are totally comfortable with them.

 25.

Lesson 4

Popping Technique

Apart from thumb slapping, the other essential part of the slap bass style is the use of the **finger popping** technique. This technique is usually done with the index finger (i) but the middle finger (m) is also sometimes used. The technique is performed by putting the end of the finger slightly under the string and then pulling it upwards and away, allowing the string to snap back against the fretboard, thus producing the sound. A combination of arm and wrist rotation is used to achieve this technique. Study the photos below and listen to the following example to hear the sound produced by popping. The popping technique is indicated in the notation by the letter **P** written above or below the note.

Finger ready to pop note

Pull up and rotate wrist

 26.

To begin with, try popping the open G and D strings as shown in the following example.

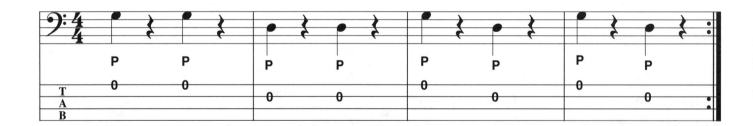

 27.

The next step is to combine the slapping and popping techniques. Take this slowly at first and use your metronome to make sure you are keeping good time.

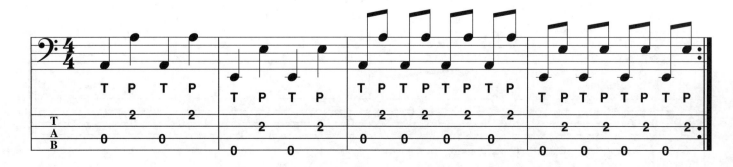

Most slap bass lines use a combination of slapping and popping. In general the lower notes are slapped and the higher notes are popped, but this is not always the case. Once you can co-ordinate the slapping and popping techniques using eighth notes, you are ready to play actual bass lines using these techniques. The following line which uses **octaves** has been used in many disco songs and will probably sound familiar to you. An **octave** is the distance between a note and its next repeat higher or lower after passing all the other letter names used for notes (**E** to **E**, **C#** to **C#** , **D** to **D**, etc). If you are unfamiliar with octaves, see **10 Easy Lessons for Bass**.

 **28.**

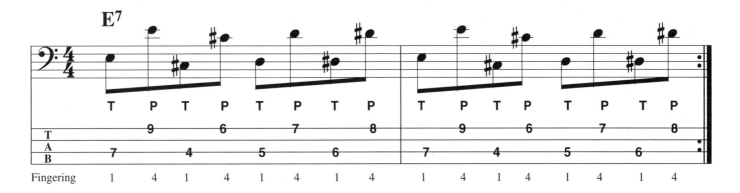

It is important to be able to comfortably use both the slapping and popping techniques on or between any beat of a bar. The following exercises should help you gain control of this. Once again, use your metronome and listen carefully as you play to make sure all your notes are strong and even. These examples are on the first and third strings, but it is important to play them on the second and fourth strings as well.

 **29.**

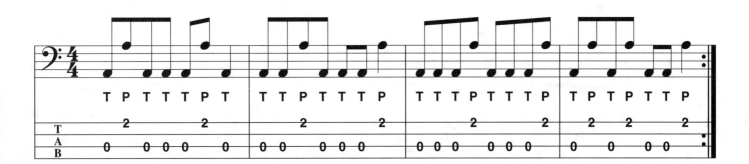

 **30.**

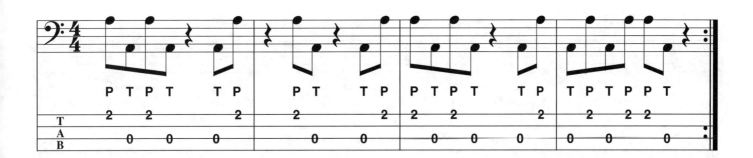

The Eighth Rest

 This is an **eighth rest**.
It indicates **half a beat of silence**.

 **31.**

The use of eighth rests on the beat is a common way of achieving syncopated rhythms. Practice this example slowly with a metronome and count out loud as you play. Once you are comfortable with the rhythm, try playing it along with the recording.

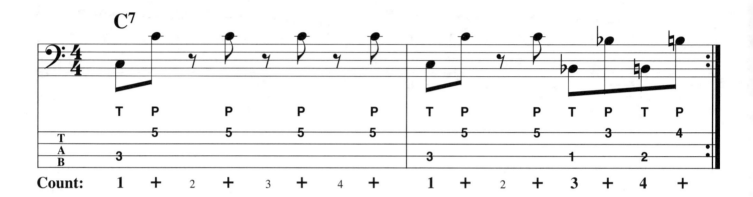

Here are some more bass lines which make use of eighth rests. Practice each one slowly until you can play it from memory and then try playing it along with the recording.

 32.

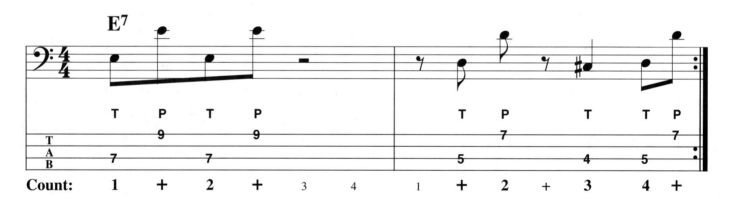

 33.

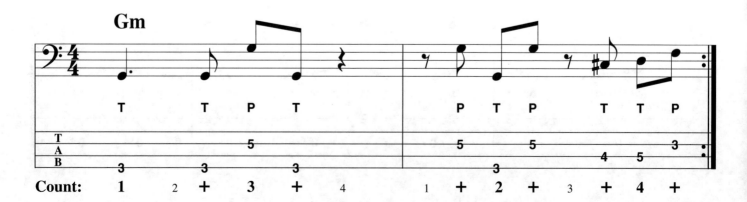

The Tie

In traditional notation, a **tie** is a curved line that connects two notes with the **same** position on the staff. A tie indicates that you play the **first** note only, and to hold it for the length of both notes. A tie is not necessary in Tab notation where you can just follow the count. The use of ties is another common way of creating syncopated rhythms.

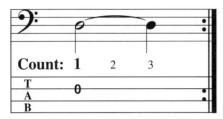

Play the D note and hold it for
3 counts

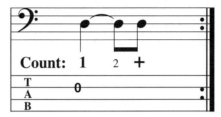

Play the D note and hold it for
$1\frac{1}{2}$ counts

A tie is necessary if a note is to be held over a bar line, as in the following bass line. In this example, the tied notes coincide with the chord changes. Notice that the bass line moves to the root note half a beat before beat 1 or beat 3 on these chord changes. This method of playing is sometimes called giving the rhythm a "push".

 **34.**

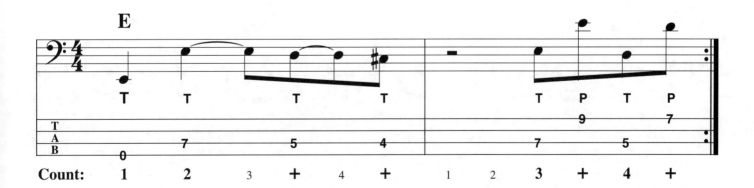

 35.

Here is another riff which makes use of ties.

Lesson 5

Articulation

The term **articulation** refers to the way notes are played and how long they are held for. Common examples of articulation are **legato** and **staccato**. Legato means that the notes are played smoothly. If there is no word or symbol telling you how to play a note, you can assume it is to be played legato. **Staccato** means that a note is to be played short and separate from other notes (the opposite of legato). Staccato is indicated by a dot placed above or below a note as shown here.

 **36.**

The notes in the first bar of this example are played legato, while the second bar is played staccato. To play a note staccato, lift the left hand finger off the fret (but not totally off the string) as soon as the note has been played.

Occasionally all the notes in a bass line are played staccato, but it is more common that some are played legato while others are staccato. In many bass lines, the use of staccato notes can add extra drive to the rhythm as demonstrated in the following example. In the first two bars all the notes are played legato. The third and fourth contain exactly the same notes, but some of them are played staccato. Notice how this helps to drive the line forward and adds life to it.

 **37.**

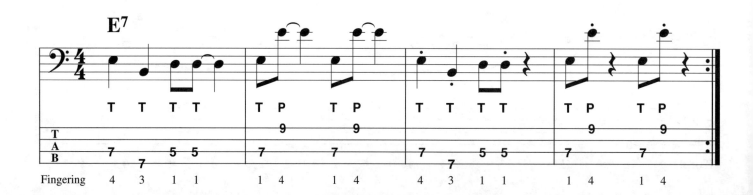

To become a good bass player, it is essential to have control over the way you articulate notes and to be able to choose the right articulations for a particular song. The following examples will give you some ideas about how to use staccato and legato in your playing. In example 38 all the notes on the beat (the slapped notes) are played legato, while the notes off the beat (the popped notes) are played staccato.

 38.

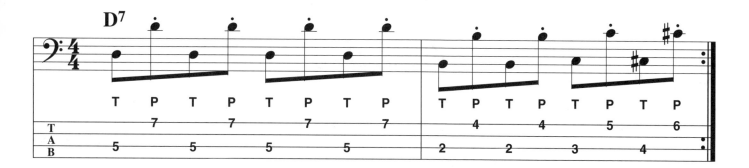

 **39.**

This time the notes on the beat (slapped) are played staccato and the notes off the beat (popped) are legato. Listen to the difference this makes to the feel of the line even though the notes are the same.

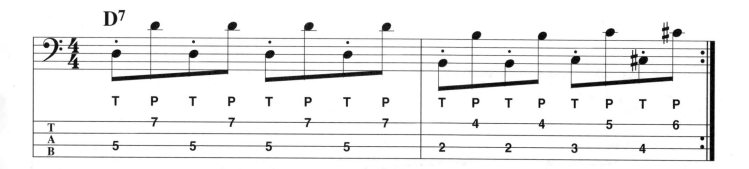

 **40.**

In many bass lines the pattern of legato and staccato notes is not so regular, as in the following example. Experiment with these articulations in your own bass lines as they can make a big difference to the way your playing sounds.

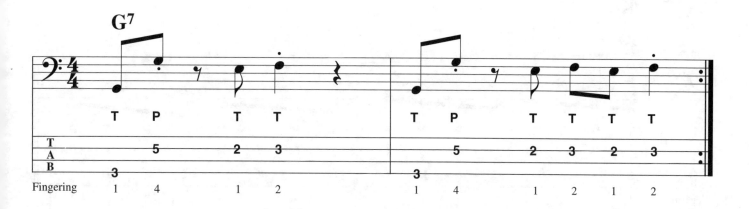

Ghost Notes

Another important type of articulation is the **ghost note** (sometimes called a **percussive** or **dampened** note). This is a note that has no particular pitch and is a more rhythmic technique of playing. It has a percussive sound and is achieved by the **left hand** lightly touching the string while the right hand plays the string. No fingers are pressed down on the neck when playing ghost notes. A ghost note is indicated by an **X** instead of a notehead.

Ghost note indicated by X instead of notehead.

 41.

In this example, the first finger of the left hand plays the G note and then relaxes up off the fret each time a ghost note is played. The second, third and fourth fingers come to rest on the string each time a ghost note is played and then move off the string while the G note is being played. Practice the technique slowly at first until you are comfortable with it.

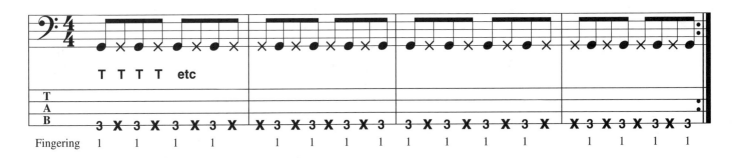

Here are a couple of bass lines demonstrating the use of ghost notes.

 **42.**

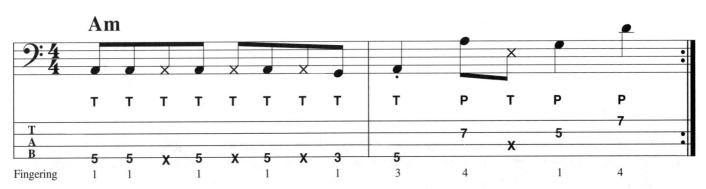

 **43.**

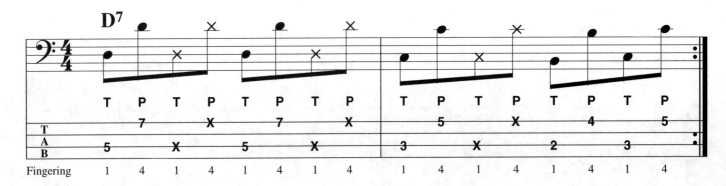

Lesson 6

Sixteenth Note Rhythms

 This is a **sixteenth note**.
It lasts for **one quarter** of a beat.
There are **four** sixteenth notes in one beat.
There are **16** sixteenth notes in one bar of $\frac{4}{4}$ time.

Two sixteenth notes joined together.

Four sixteenth notes joined together.

Count: 1   e   +   a

Say: one 'ee'   and   'ah'

 44. How to Count 16th Notes

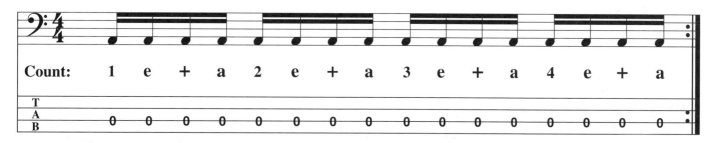

Here are some exercises to help you become comfortable using sixteenth notes with both slapping and popping. As with any new note value or technique, take them slowly at first, count out loud as you play, and use a metronome.

 45.

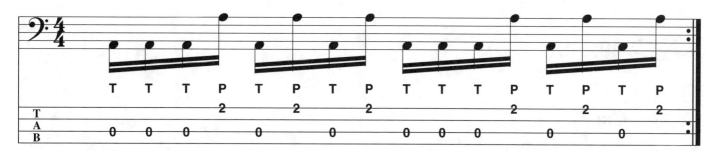

 **46.**

Common Sixteenth Note Figures

Sixteenth notes are commonly used within a beat in conjunction with eighth notes. The following example demonstrates two common rhythm figures combining sixteenth notes and eighth notes.

 47.

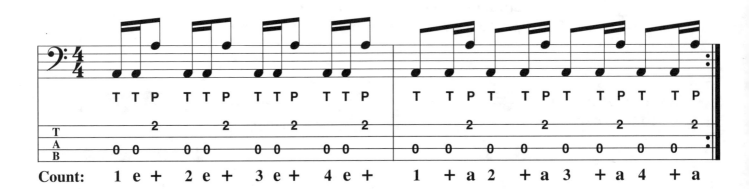

Here are some bass lines which make use of these two rhythms.

 48.

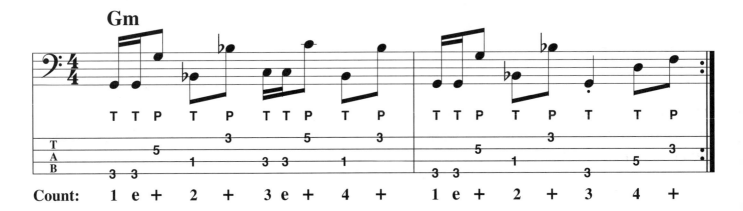

 **49.**

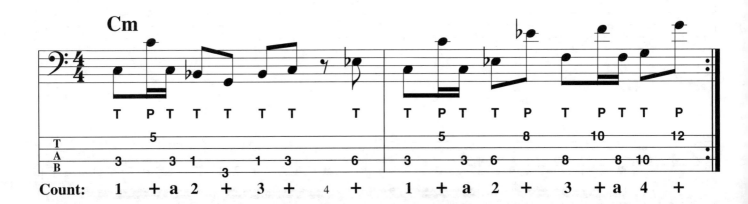

Here are four more important 16th note figures. Each of these rhythms is played with the right thumb (**T**). The first one contains a dotted eighth note. Remember that a dot increases the value of a note by half, so the dotted eighth note is worth three quarters of a beat.

 **50.**

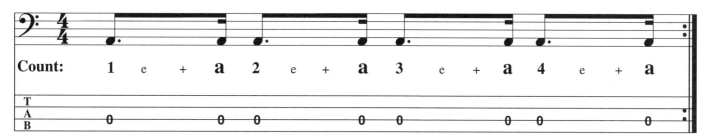

 **51.**

This one contains two sixteenth notes and an eighth note. You may find these rhythms difficult at first but they are all important, so stick with it. Use a metronome as you practice them and count out loud as you play. If you are tapping your foot, make sure it taps only on each beat and not in between.

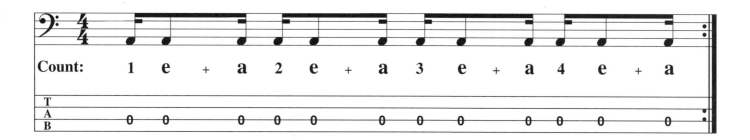

 **52.**

The next two rhythms involve the use of sixteenth note rests. Once again take them slowly at first, count out loud and use a metronome.

 **53.**

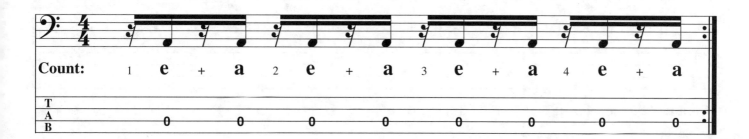

Rhythm Studies

To help you become more comfortable with sixteenth note figures and work them into your playing, here are some rhythm studies which involve both slapping and popping. As with the previous examples, play them slowly at first and count out loud as you play. Don't forget to use your metronome, and tap your foot on each beat.

 **54.**

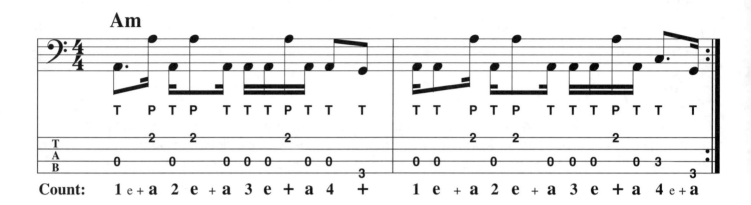

 **55.**

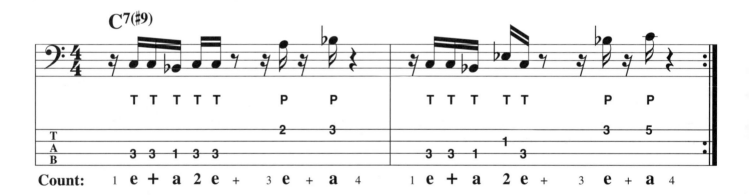

 **56.**

Here is one which makes use of ties.

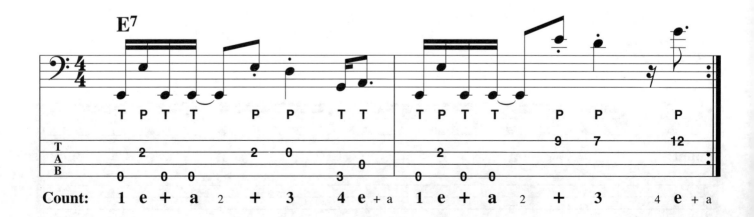

Analyzing Sixteenth Note Rhythms

In a bar of sixteenth notes in $\frac{4}{4}$ time, there are **16** different positions for notes within the bar. This means that it can be difficult to identify exactly where some of the notes fall in some bass lines. There is a simple system for identifying any note's position in a bar by naming notes off the beat according to which beat they come directly after. The system works as follows. The first beat is **1**, the second note of the first group of four is called the "**e of one**" the third note of the first group is called the "**and of one**", and the fourth note of the first group is called the "**a of one**". The system then continues through the bar - **2**, **e of 2**, **and of 2**, **a of 2**, etc.

A good way to become familiar with this system is to play constant sixteenth notes with the right hand and to articulate the rhythms with the left hand, playing the rests as ghost notes as shown in the example below. Once again all the notes are played with thumb slaps (**T**). To help you clearly identify where the notes which are not ghosted fall, accent these notes with your voice as you play. In this example these notes occur on **1**, the **e of 2**, the **and of 3** and the **a of 4**. Use this system to analyze any rhythm you have trouble playing.

 **57.**

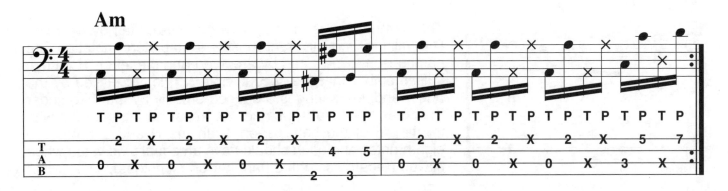

As with eighth note based lines, it is common to use ghost notes in lines based on 16th notes. Here are some exercises to help you become more comfortable with ghost notes in 16th based lines.

 **58.**

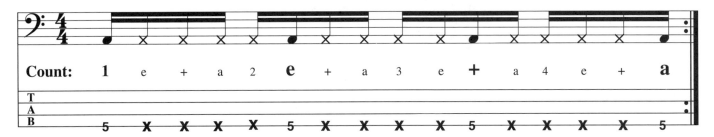

 **59.**

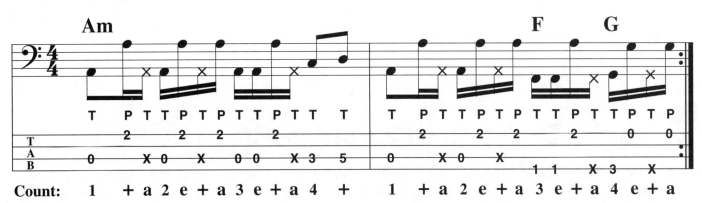

Lesson 7

Left Hand Techniques

Apart from scale positions, almost everything you have learnt up to this point has been mostly focused on the right hand. However, there are several important left hand techniques which can make your playing sound more interesting and expressive, as well as enabling you to play things which are not possible without these techniques. The first of these involves flattening the first finger across several strings and pressing down behind a fret as shown in the following photo. This is called making a **bar** with the finger (similar to a guitarist playing bar chords). When playing the following example, keep the first finger bar down to play all notes at the 5th fret.

Use first finger as a bar across strings

 **60.**

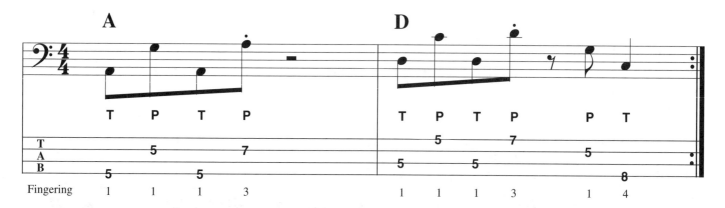

The Hammer-on (H)

A "**hammer-on**" refers to the technique of sounding a note without actually playing the string with the right hand. The sound is produced by striking the string with one of the left hand fingers. In the following example, only the **D** note is slapped, and the **third** finger "hammers-on" firmly to produce the sound of the **E** note, as shown in the photos on the following page.

 **61.**

The **hammer-on** is indicated on the music staff by a curved line joining two different notes. In tablature notation the hammer-on is indicated by a curved and the letter "**H**" above it. Remember that the second note (E), is not played by the right hand; the sound is produced entirely by the third finger "hammering-on" to the string. You must be very careful with the timing of the hammer-on. Both the D and E notes are eighth notes and each should have an equal time value when played (regardless of the hammer-on technique).

Play D note (slap)

Hammer-on to sound E note

 62.

Here is an exercise to help you develop the use of hammer-ons. It is shown here on the 4th and 3rd strings, but should continue on the 2nd and 1st strings. It should be practiced many times in succession both ascending and descending.

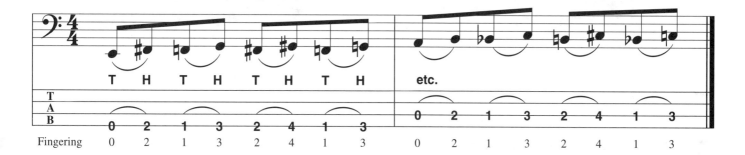

 **63.**

Here is a riff which makes frequent use of hammer-ons.

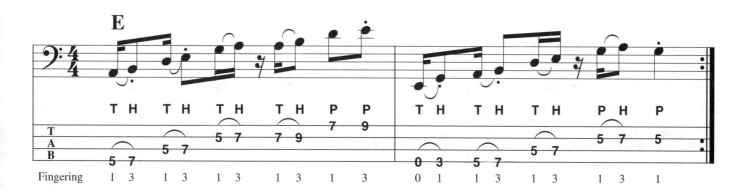

 **64.**

This one uses both hammer-ons and a first finger bar.

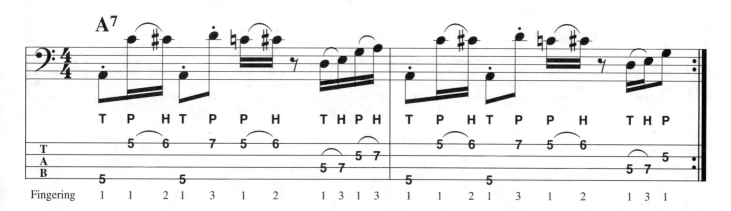

The Pull-off (PO)

The **pull-off** is like a reverse hammer-on, i.e. the first note is played with the right hand and the second note sound is created by the finger pulling off the string. In the example below the **E** note is played by the right hand and the **D** note sound is created by the **third** finger pulling off the string. The pull-off is indicated by the letters **PO** and a curved line. In some music a pull-off is indicated by the letter **P** by itself, but **PO** is used here to distinguish the pull-off from popped notes.

Play E note (slap)

Pull-off to sound D note

 65.

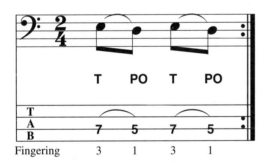

Here is a riff which makes use of pull-offs. As with earlier examples, be sure to damp out any extra unwanted sounds.

 **66.**

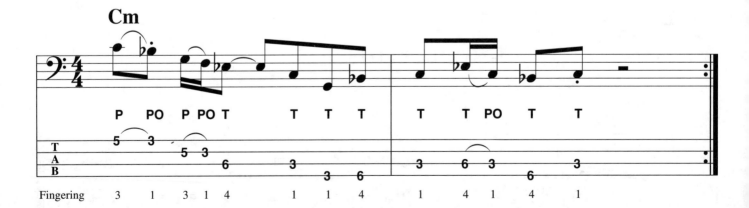

The Slide (S)

The **slide** is a technique which involves a finger moving along the string to its new note. The finger maintains pressure on the string, so that a continuous sound is produced until the desired note is reached. The left hand moves from one note to the next, upwards or downwards on the fretboard. The slide is indicated by a line joining two notes.

Only the first note is played by the pick or the right hand fingers, the second one is entirely produced by the left hand finger sliding up or down the fretboard. The length of the slide can be one fret (as in the example on the right) or as many frets as you wish. Practice sliding your finger up and down the fretboard. Play only the first note.

The slide is indicated on the music staff by a line leading up to the note you are sliding to. In tablature notation the slide is indicated by a line with the letter **S** above it. The following bass lines make use of slides.

67.

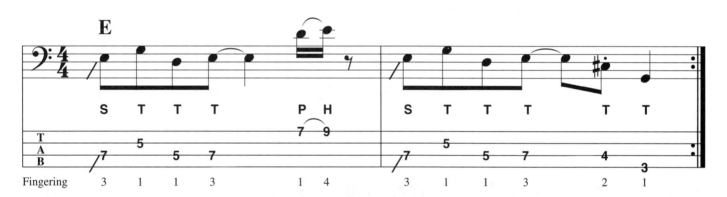

68.

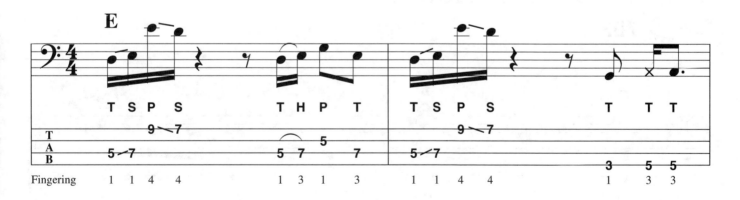

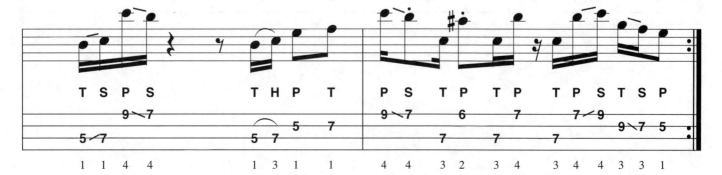

Grace Notes

To create a different feel with a hammer-on, it can be played faster. Compare the following:

The quick hammer-on is also called a **grace note**. In traditional music notation the grace note is a smaller size with a line through the stem. The grace note is played just before the beat of the hammered on note. Quick slides can also be described as grace notes. The following example demonstrates grace notes played as quick hammer-ons and also one played as a quick slide.

 **69.**

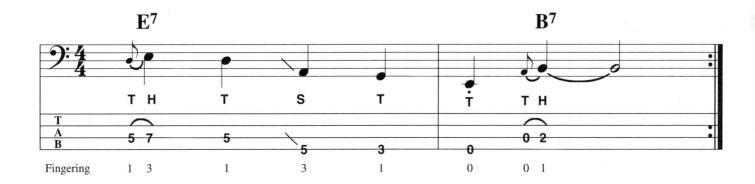

The Trill (Tr)

The trill is a rapid succession of hammer-ons and pull-offs where only the first note is played by the right hand. A trill is indicated by the letters **tr** written above or below the notes. Listen to the following example on the CD to hear the effect of the trill.

 **70.**

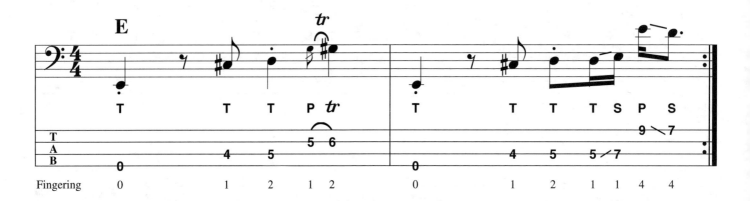

To finish this lesson, here are some bass lines which make use of all the techniques you have just learnt. Experiment with these techniques and create some of your own lines.

 **71.**

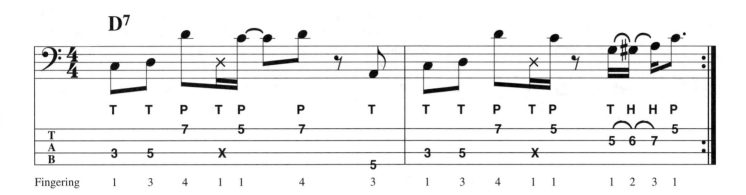

 **72.**

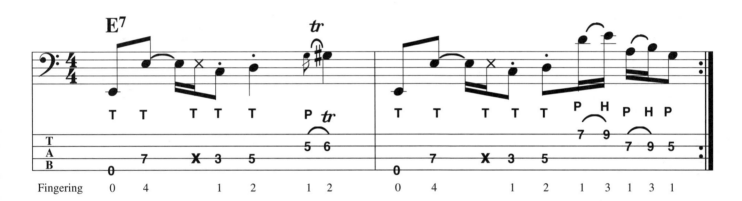

 **73.**

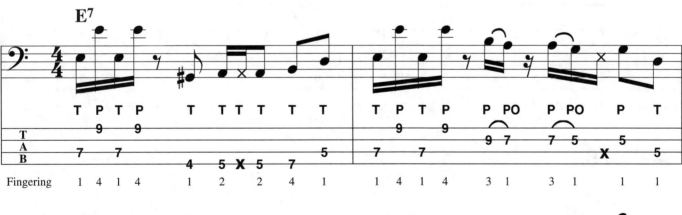

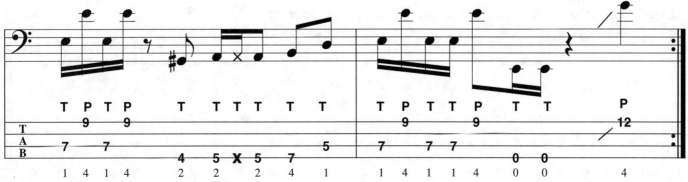

Lesson 8

The Triplet

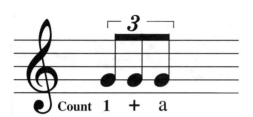
Count 1 + a

An eighth note **triplet** is a group of **three** evenly spaced notes played within one beat. Eighth note triplets are indicated by three eighth notes grouped together with the numeral **3** above them. Each part of the triplet is worth a third of a beat. Triplets are easy to understand once you have heard them played. Listen to example 74 on the CD to hear the effect of triplets.

 ### 74. How to Count Triplets

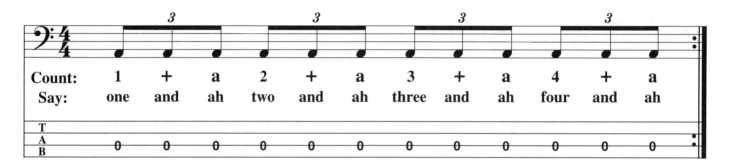

Count:	1	+	a	2	+	a	3	+	a	4	+	a
Say:	one	and	ah	two	and	ah	three	and	ah	four	and	ah

Here are a couple of exercises to help you become more familiar with triplets.

 ### 75.

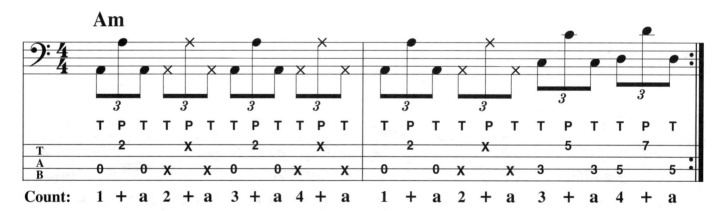

 ### 76.

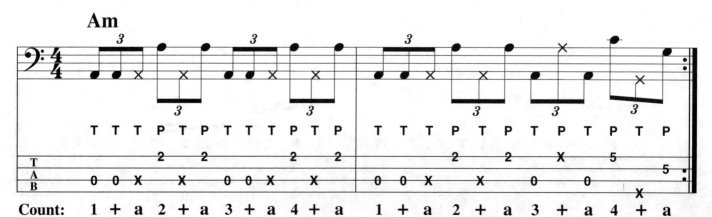

Swing Rhythms

A **swing rhythm** can be created by tying the first two notes of the triplet group together.

77.

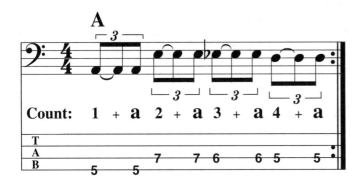

 **78.**

The two eighth note triplets tied together in example 77 can be replaced by a quarter note.

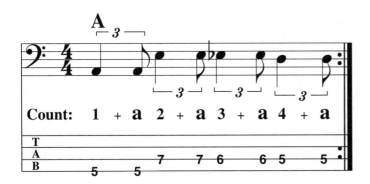

To simplify notation, it is common to replace the ♩♩ with ♩ ♪,

and to write at the start of the piece ♫ = ♩ ♪ as illustrated below in example 79.

79. ♫ = ♩ ♪

Here are some lines which use swung eighth notes as well as triplets. This first one uses **lead-in notes** (also called pickup notes). These are notes which come before the first full bar. When lead-in notes are used, the last bar is often incomplete, as the lead-in notes are added to the count.

80.

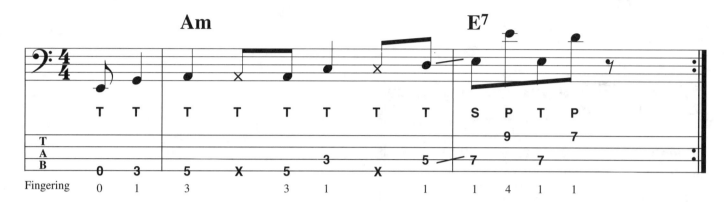

81.

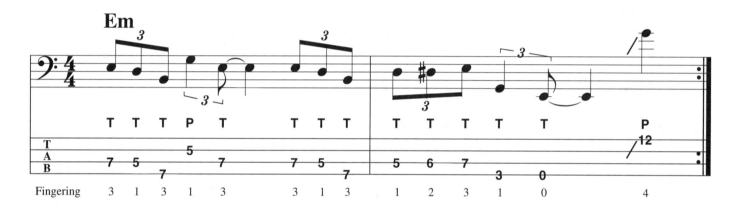

The Sixteenth Note Triplet

Triplets can be created on any note value. A sixteenth note triplet is three sixteenth notes played evenly across the space usually taken by two sixteenth notes. This means that the triplet grouping lasts for the same duration as an eighth note. It is common for two sixteenth note triplets to occur together as a group of six notes across one quarter note beat. The example below demonstrates sixteenth note triplets. As with previous note values, practice it with your metronome and be sure to keep your notes even. To count a sixteenth note triplet, say **ta ka ta**, for two across a beat, say **ta ka ta ta ka ta**.

82.

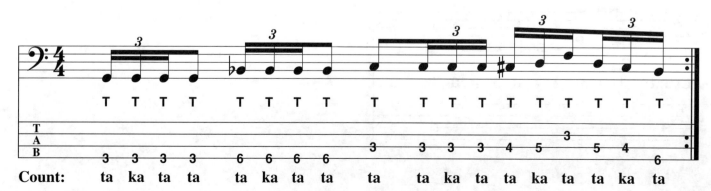

Swinging Sixteenth Notes

Like eighth notes, it is possible to swing sixteenth notes by playing the first and third notes of the triplet grouping. Swung 16th rhythms are common in Funk, Hip-Hop and Rock which is influenced by these styles. Try swinging a bar of constant 16th notes on one note until you are comfortable with the rhythm, and then try the following lines which make use of swung 16ths. You should also experiment with swinging the 16ths on other lines which you already know.

**83.**

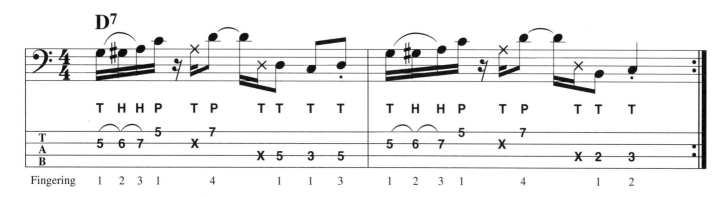

**84.**

Notice the descending slide at the end of the final note in this example. This is called a **trail-off**, or **fall-off**, which is an expressive technique used by many instrumentalists. Rather than sliding to a specific note, the trail-off begins with a specific note and then trails away to an indefinite pitch. Experiment with this technique when creating your own lines.

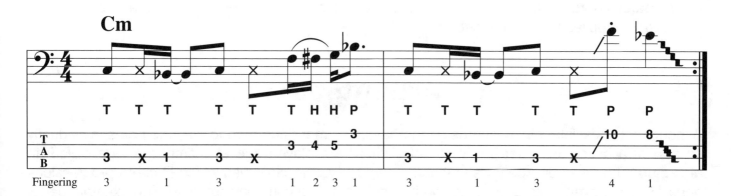

**85.**

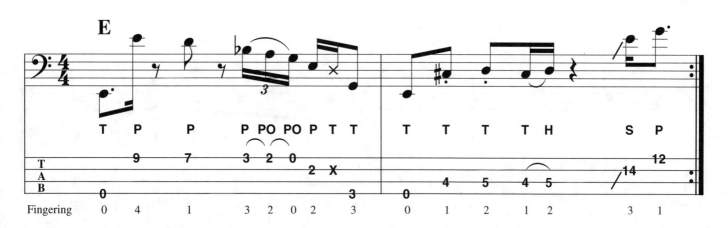

Lesson 9

Understanding Chords

A **chord** is a group of 3 or more notes played simultaneously. Different types of chords can be formed by using different combinations of notes. The most common type of chord is the **major chord**. All major chords contain three notes, taken from the major scale of the same letter name. (If you are not familiar with the major scale, see *10 Easy Lessons for Bass*). These three notes are the 1 (root note), 3 (third) and 5 (fifth) degrees of the major scale, so the **chord formula** for the major chord is:

1   3   5

Chord Symbol

The C Major Chord

Notes in Chord

C	E	G
1	3	5

The C major chord is constructed from the C major scale. Using the above chord formula on the C major scale below, it can be seen that the C major chord contains the notes C, E and G.

C Major Scale

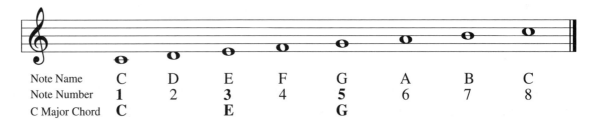

Note Name	C	D	E	F	G	A	B	C
Note Number	1	2	3	4	5	6	7	8
C Major Chord	C		E		G			

The chord symbol for a major chord is just the letter name of the chord. E.g, the chord symbol for the **C major** chord is **C**. It is common practice to refer to a C major chord as the C chord. This abbreviation applies to all major chords.

Arpeggios

Although it is possible to play chords on the bass, it is more common to play the notes individually as part of a bass line. When the notes of a chord are played one at a time, they are called an **arpeggio**. The value of arpeggios is that they enable you to play lines which fit chord progressions perfectly, since every note of an arpeggio is a note of the accompanying chord. The example below demonstrates a **C major arpeggio** which consists of the notes **C**, **E** and **G**. These are the **root**, **third** and **fifth** of a **C major chord**.

 **86.0**

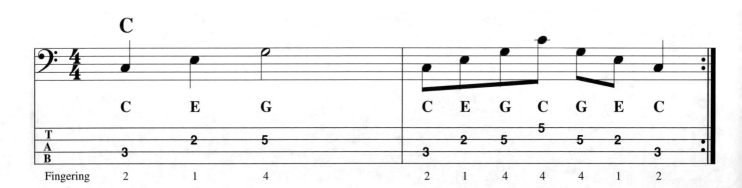

Here are two common arpeggio patterns for any major chord. The first diagram shows the Root, third and fifth, while the second diagram shows the repeat of the root note an octave higher. They are shown here beginning on the fourth string, but can also be used beginning on the third string.

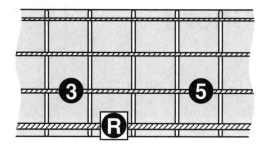
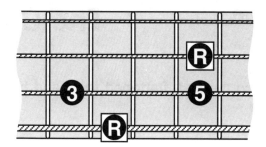

Inversions

Once you have the correct notes for a chord they can be arranged in any order. These various arrangements of the notes within a chord are called **inversions**. E.g. a **C** chord could be played **C E G** (called **root position**), or **E G C** (**first inversion**), or **G C E** (**second inversion**). The use of inversions opens up many new fingering possibilities all over the fretboard. It is worth learning all inversions of each arpeggio, as this enables you to identify all the degrees of the chord (called chord tones) more easily, which means you can respond quickly to what is being played by other musicians you are playing with regardless of the harmony. If you know the notes and inversions of chords well, it also makes it a lot easier to improvise your own bass lines in any position on the fretboard. It is also recommended that you learn at least a bit of basic keyboard or guitar so you get used to hearing the sound of all of the notes of chords together instead of one at a time. Most of the great bass players also have an excellent knowledge of keyboard harmony.

Upside down Arpeggios

Because it is the role of the bass to provide the bottom end of the sound of the band, it is usually best to stay on the lower part of the neck, or at least on the lower strings, for most of the time. If you play too much high up on the neck on the first and second strings, the sound gets thin and the punch of the bass is lost. Remember that the bass is a foundation instrument, providing the drive of the groove and stating the basis of the harmony of a song. A useful technique for enabling you to stay in one place lower down the neck is the use of "upside down' arpeggios. This means that you go **down** from the root to the third instead of up, as demonstrated in the following example.

 **86.1**

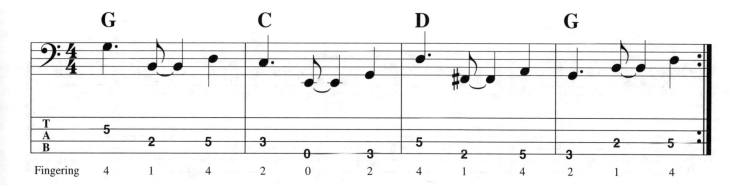

Minor Chords

1 ♭3 5

The C Minor Chord

Notes in Chord

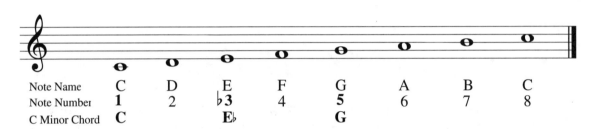

By taking the first, **flattened third** and fifth degrees of a C major scale, a **C minor** chord can be created.

C Major Scale

Note Name	C	D	E	F	G	A	B	C
Note Number	**1**	2	**♭3**	4	**5**	6	7	8
C Minor Chord	**C**		**E♭**		**G**			

Minor Arpeggios

For every type of chord there is a corresponding arpeggio. This means there are major, minor, augmented, diminished, dominant seventh and minor seventh arpeggios among others. Shown below is a **C minor arpeggio** which consists of the notes **C**, **E♭** and **G** which are the **root**, **flattened third** and **fifth** of a **C minor chord**.

 87.0.

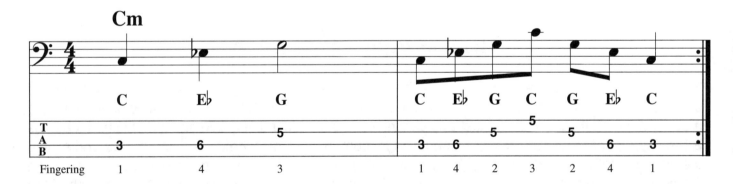

 87.1

Here is a bass line which makes use of a C minor arpeggio. Remember that as long as you play the correct notes for any arpeggio, these notes can be arranged in any order.

Seventh Chords

C7

The C Seventh Chord (C7)

Notes in Chord

C	E	G	B♭
1	3	5	♭7

Another common chord type used in Rock is the **seventh chord**, (sometimes called the dominant seventh chord). Seventh chords consist of four notes taken from the major scale of the same letter name. These notes are the first (1), third (3), fifth (5) and flattened seventh (♭7) notes of the major scale, so the **chord formula** for the seventh chord is:

$$1 \qquad 3 \qquad 5 \qquad ♭7$$

A flattened seventh (♭7) is created by lowering the seventh note of the major scale by one semitone. This is the same ♭7 note that is found in the Blues scale. Notice that the seventh chord is simply a major chord with a flattened seventh note added. Shown below is a **C7** arpeggio.

 **88.0**

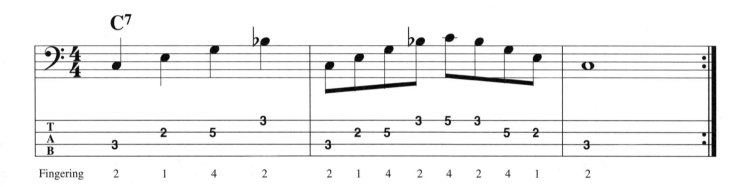

 88.1

Here is a bass line which makes use of a C7 arpeggio. Once again, remember that as long as you play the correct notes for any arpeggio, these notes can be arranged in any order.

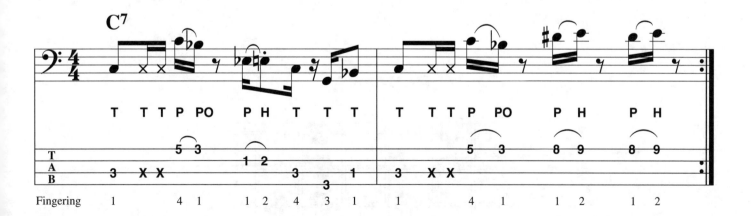

Understanding The Fretboard

You will have noticed that many of the scales, arpeggios and bass lines you have learned can be played in more than one place on the fretboard. Altogether there are five basic moveable fingering positions which cover the whole fretboard when linked up end to end. These fingering positions can be applied to any type of scale or arpeggio. The most important element to learning these positions is **memorizing the positions of the root notes**. You have already learned to play the Blues scale in two of these fingering patterns in lesson 2. The diagrams below demonstrate the five basic fingerings for the Blues scale. They are shown here in the key of G but are moveable to all 12 keys represented by the notes of the chromatic scale. Learn to play each fingering one at a time, memorizing the scale degrees and in particular, the positions of the root notes.

Pattern 1

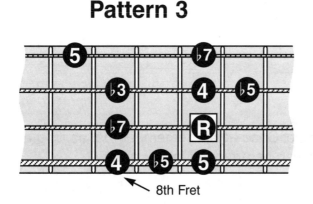

Pattern 2

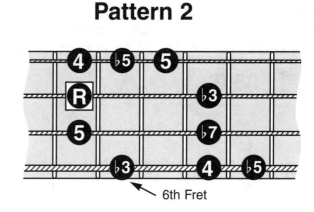

Pattern 3

Pattern 4

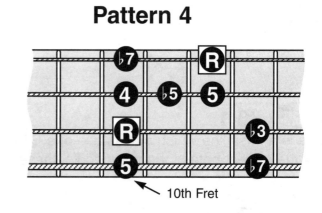

Pattern 5

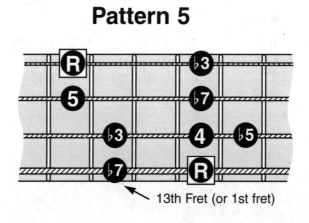

Here are some sample base lines derived from the new patterns you have just learned. The first of these comes from pattern 2. Memorize each one and transpose it to several other keys.

 **89.0.**

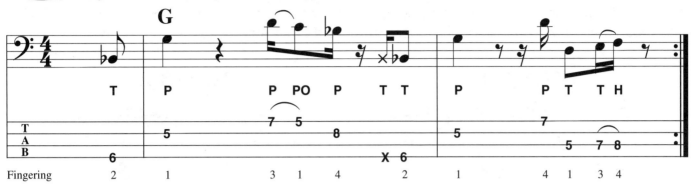

 **89.1**

This one comes from pattern 3. Notice the 16th note triplet in the second bar.

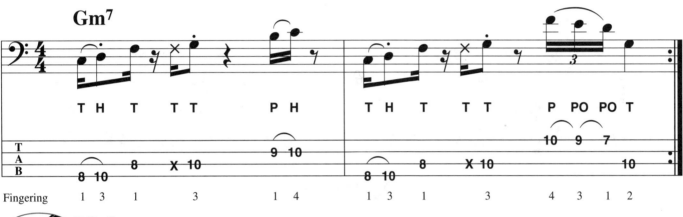

 **89.2**

Here is a line derived from pattern 4.

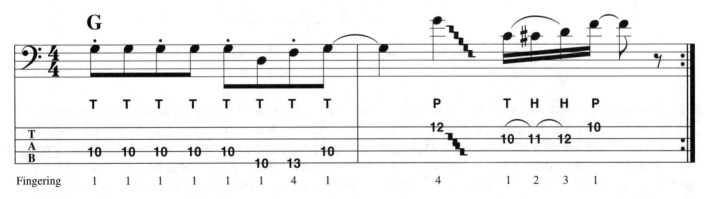

 **89.3**

And finally, one from pattern 5. After this, pattern 1 repeats an octave higher than it was at the 3rd fret.

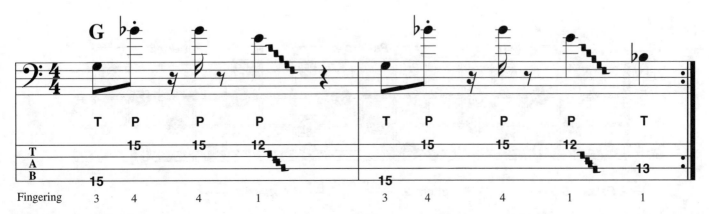

Five Patterns For Arpeggios

As mentioned earlier in this lesson, the five basic fingering patterns apply to any type of scale or arpeggio. Shown below are the five patterns of a **G7** arpeggio. As with all new patterns you learn, transpose them to several other keys once you have them memorized.

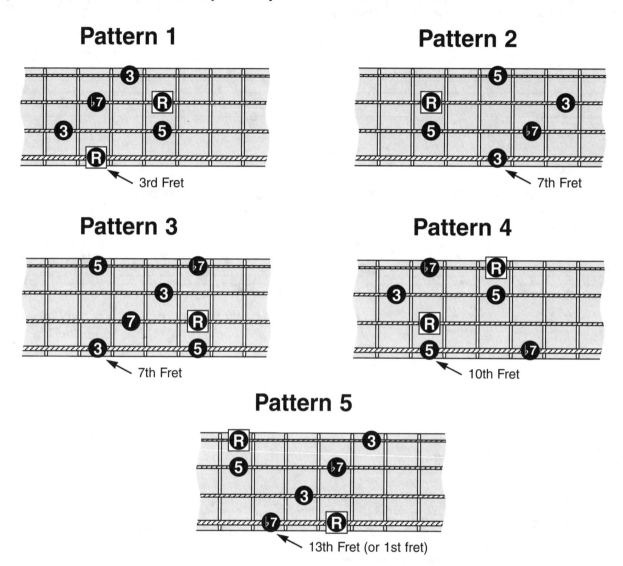

The following diagram shows the positions of the root notes from all five patterns. The positions of these root notes never change, regardless of the type of scale or arpeggio being played. The positions of the other notes may change, but the root notes don't. Because of this, they form a framework around which any bass line can be built. For this reason, it is essential to memorise the positions of these root notes. Try visualizing them with your eyes closed, or while you are away from the bass (e.g. while waiting for a bus). Name the positions (string and fret number) of the notes in a particular key until you can do it instantly. When you can do this, move on to another key. Keep working at this bit by bit until you know all the root note positions for all 12 keys.

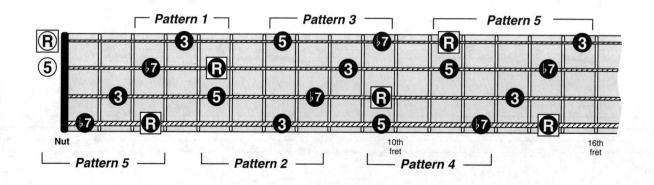

Applying Scale and Chord Formulas

Once you know the positions of the root notes all over the neck, the next step is to learn how all the other notes of the chromatic scale relate to these root notes in each position. This is a great exercise, because once you can find all the notes in each position, you can quickly work out a fingering for any type of scale or arpeggio anywhere on the neck. All you have to do is learn the scale or chord formula (a particular set of degrees) and you can instantly play it. Shown below is a diagram of pattern 1 in the key of **C** containing all the degrees of the chromatic scale up as far as the 5th degree on the first string. Play through it and name the degrees as you play. The diagram shows the degrees and the notation shows the fingering. Notice that degrees with two possible names (e.g. #2 or b3) are named as flats rather than sharps. This is because most scale and chord formulas tend to use flattened degrees rather than sharpened degrees. E.g. a minor seventh chord contains the degrees **1**, **b3**, **5** and **b7** and a Blues scale contains the degrees **1**, **b3**, **4**, **b5**, **♮5**, and **b7**.

Pattern 1

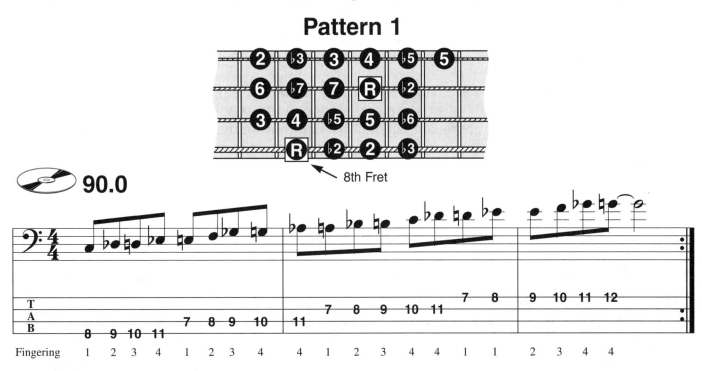

When you are confident you know the positions of all the notes as they relate to the framework of the root notes, you are ready to try working out some fingerings for specific scales based on their individual formula. The example given below is the minor pentatonic scale. As the name suggests, this scale contains five notes which are **1**, **b3**, **4**, **5** and **b7**. Notice that this is simply the Blues scale with the flattened 5th degree left out. Because you already know the Blues scale, it should be easy to work out all five fingerings for the minor pentatonic scale. Experiment with it and make up some of your own bass lines from it.

Minor Pentatonic Formula = 1 b3 4 5 b7

C Minor Pentatonic = C Eb F G Bb

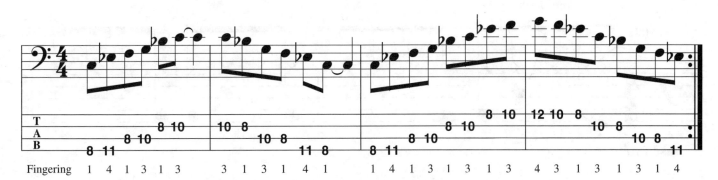

Lesson 10

Working With a Drummer

Learning to fit your part with other instruments is very important for all bass players. It is especially important to be able to play well with a drummer, as the bass and drums form what is known as the **rhythm section**. Together, the rhythm section provide the rhythmic and harmonic foundation for the whole band. While a guitarist or piano player can play solo, the bass is really made for playing with a band.

When you are playing with other musicians, the most important thing is to listen to each other and try to respond to what the other players are doing. In an ideal band, everyone is equally responsible for keeping good time but in reality, many musicians (especially guitarists who play by ear only) neglect the study of rhythm and beat subdivisions and rely on the rhythm section to keep good time and indicate what is happening rhythmically. While a singer or horn player has time to breathe between phrases and a guitarist or keyboard player leaves space between lines or chords, the drummer and bass player have to play consistently to keep the groove going and feeling good.

Because the bass and drums work so closely together, it is worth learning a bit about drum notation and drumming in general. Drum music is usually written in the spaces of the bass staff, including the space above the staff, to represent different parts of the drum kit. The most commonly used system is shown below. Notice that cymbals are notated with an **X** in a similar manner to ghost notes on the bass.

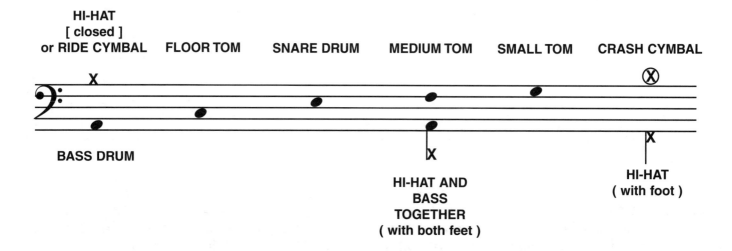

The following example demonstrates a simple Rock beat on the drums. Follow the notation as you listen to the recording and then try reading the notation without the recording and imagining the sounds of the drums as you follow the notes.

 **91.0**

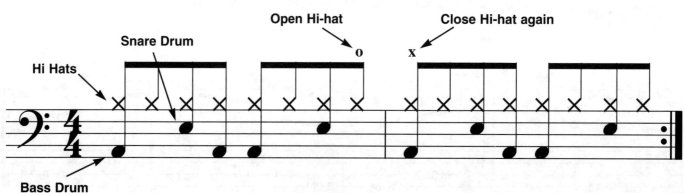

If you were going to create a bass line to go with this drum beat, the first thing you would look at is the bass drum pattern. Because of the type of patterns the bass drum plays, as well as its low sound, the bass and bass drum often "lock in" together as shown in the following example.

91.1

Another common point where the bass and drums often connect is where the snare drum is played. Because of its higher sound, the snare drum sounds good when played along with popped notes, as shown below. Notice that the bass plays along with some of the snare drum notes but not all of them.

91.2

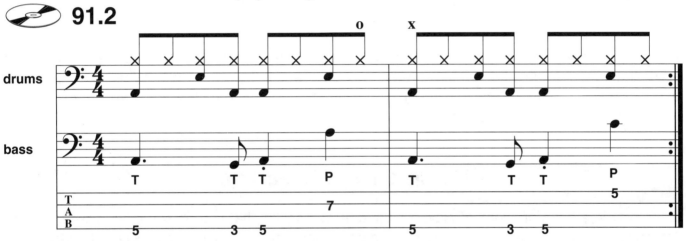

If you wanted to change the bass line to make it sound more interesting, there are a couple of things you could look for in the drum part which might give you some ideas. The first is the open hi-hat on the "and of 4" in the first bar. This would be a good spot to put an extra bass note, because it adds interest to the line and also connects directly with the drums. The other clue here is that the hi-hat part consists of constant eighth notes, which means you could put extra notes on any of these eight points in the bar, or in between them so that the hi-hat answers the bass. Listen to the following example on the CD to hear how the new version of the bass line works with the drum part.

91.3

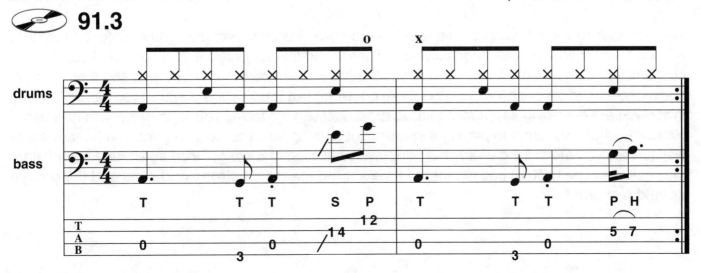

As mentioned on the previous page, it sometimes works well to have the bass play in between some of the drum parts and let the drums (e.g. snare drum) answer the bass. This also works the other way around; i.e. the bass answers the drums. Listen to the interplay between the bass and drums in the following example.

 **91.4**

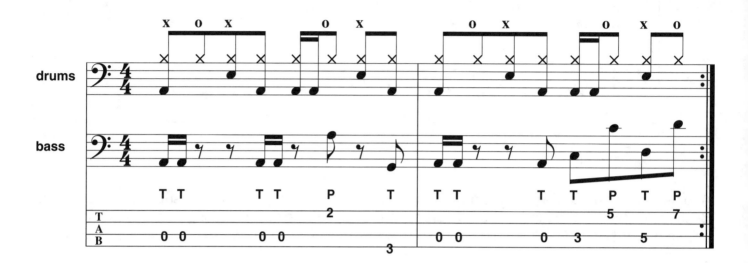

If you work together often with a drummer, you can get to the point where you each know what the other is going to do next and orchestrate the music between you as you play. When you get to this point, the bass and drums begin to sound like different parts of one multi-faceted instrument. This is the goal all rhythm section players should aim for.

Using a Drum Machine

If you play in a band or intend to play in a band, it is essential that you do some work every day on creating bass lines that work with specific drum parts. Because you can't always work with a drummer, it is a good idea to buy a **drum machine** and program your own drum beats into it. Playing along with a drum machine will improve your timing and enable you to focus on the drums more easily when you are in a band situation. Another advantage of using a drum machine is that it enables you to experiment and go through the trial and error process of working out where to play with a particular drum part and where to play in between the drum notes for each new drum beat you work with. When you play with a drum part, remember to **leave space** for the other instrumental parts instead of playing every available note in the bar. Bass players who can lock in well with a drummer without overplaying are always in demand.

When practicing parts for songs, play the basic groove over and over until you can do it easily in a relaxed manner and you feel good playing it. Then try adding a few fills and variations. If you are not comfortable doing a particular part, analyze what it is you are having difficulty with and then work on that part over and over with the drum machine, **counting out loud** as you play until you can do it easily. When you are practicing, experimentation is great because it enables you to come up with new parts. However, when you come to playing a song live, it is often better to go with parts you already know well (unless you are soloing or are in an improvised section of a song) Once again, underplay rather than overplay. **The bottom line is that the time should always be strong and solid and the groove should feel good**.

Finishing Touches

If you have worked carefully on all the techniques and concepts presented in the book, you should be well on the way to being an excellent slap bass player. To add some finishing touches to your playing, here are some more expressive techniques which will enable you to achieve more sophisticated sounds and make your playing more professional. Most of the techniques shown here are only demonstrated with one example, but you should experiment with each technique and create some of your own bass lines using them.

The Bend

The bend is achieved by "pushing" a string with the left hand fingers in the direction of the adjacent strings. This causes the note to rise in pitch. On instruments such as guitar, saxophone or harmonica, notes are most commonly bent one tone (2 frets in pitch) or one semitone (1 fret in pitch). However, on the bass it is more common to bend only a semitone (or quarter tone) because of the thickness of the strings. The examples given below use the third finger to bend the notes. You will find bending easier if the second finger also helps "push up" the string (bending the string). The bend is indicated in tablature by a curved arrow (see ex 92.0 below) and the letter **B** above it. In music notation a slur is used to connect the bent notes, so you will need to refer to the letter **B** above the tab.

In the following example, the **D** note on the 7th fret of the 1st string is bent up a semitone to an E♭ note which would usually be played at the 8th fret. This note is shown in brackets in the tab. Experience and practice will help you bend to the correct pitch. If you use light guage strings on your bass, bending will be easier.

 92.0

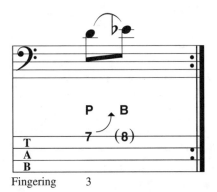

Fingering   3

Play note on 7th fret, 1st string.

Third finger bends string upwards with help of the second finger.

 92.1

Here is a bass riff which makes use of bends. Notice that the bend on the C note (5th fret, first string) with the first finger has no bracket after it. This is because it is a quarter tone bend which is a very slight bend.

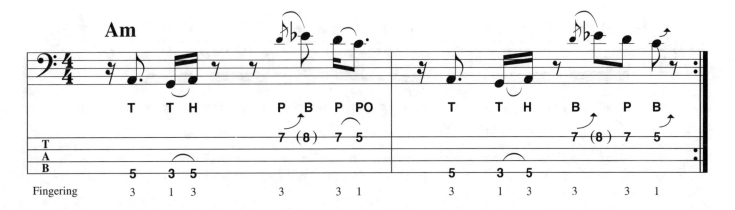

Vibrato

Vibrato is a technique where the left hand moves the fretted string rapidly up and down small distances towards adjacent strings. Vibrato helps to sustain a note and can make that note more interesting, and is mostly used on long notes or at the end of a phrase. Vibrato is indicated by a **wavy line** written above the note and tab. Vibrato can be applied to any fretted note and played by any left hand finger. Listen to the following example on the CD to hear the effect of vibrato.

 93.

Double Stops

The term **double stop** means two notes played together. This is usually done by popping notes on the first and second strings with the **m** and **i** fingers, as shown in the following example.

 94.

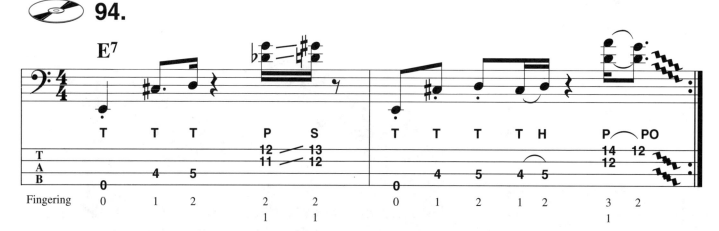

The Crosshammer

A **crosshammer** is achieved by playing a note on one string (e.g 3rd string) and hammering-on to a note on a different string (e.g. 1st string). The hammer-on must be quite firm to sound the note properly.

95.

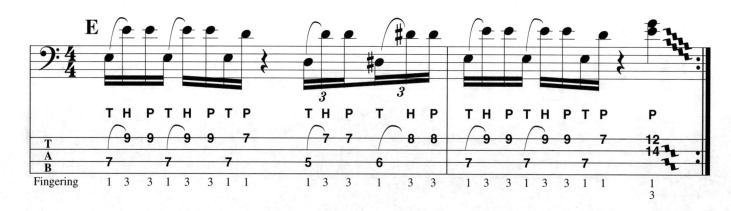

Left Hand Slap

A left **hand slap** is achieved by literally slapping the string onto the neck with the left hand. This produces a percussive effect similar to a ghost note. Left hand slaps most often occur on the 4th string, but can occur on other strings as well. A left hand slap is indicated by the letters **LS** above the tab. As with any new technique, practice it slowly at first and listen carefully to make sure your notes are clear and even.

 **96.**

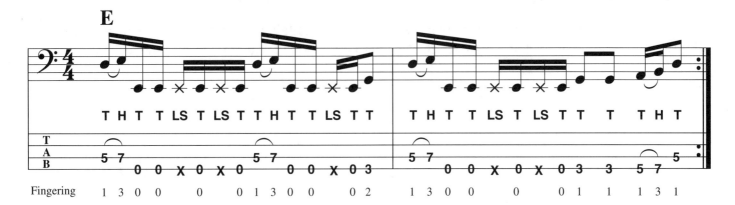

You now have all the information you need to become a great slap bass player. It's up to you to put in the persistent effort to be the best you can. Practice every day with your drum machine, count out loud with every new thing you learn, and above all, play with other musicians as often as possible. To finish things off, here is a line which contains all the new techniques presented in this lesson.

 97.

Once you know all the notes of the chromatic scale, you have covered all the starting notes for every scale and arpeggio used in music. Therefore, once you know the formula and fingerings for any scale or arpeggio, you should easily be able to play it in any key (as long as you know all the notes on the fretboard properly). To be a good musician, it is essential to be able to play equally well in all keys, because throughout the course of your musical life you will be required to play in them all, and often at a moments notice. If you are playing with a singer, you will have to play songs in whatever key suits their particular voice. That could be **F♯** or **D♭** for example. Keyboard players tend to like the keys of **C**, **F** and **G**, while **E** and **A** are fairly common keys for guitar. Horn players like flat keys such as **F**, **B♭** and **E♭**. So you can see why it is essential to learn to play equally well in every key.

A good way to learn to play in all keys is to use the **key cycle** (also called the cycle of 5ths or cycle of 4ths) as a reference. It contains the names of all the keys and is fairly easy to memorize.

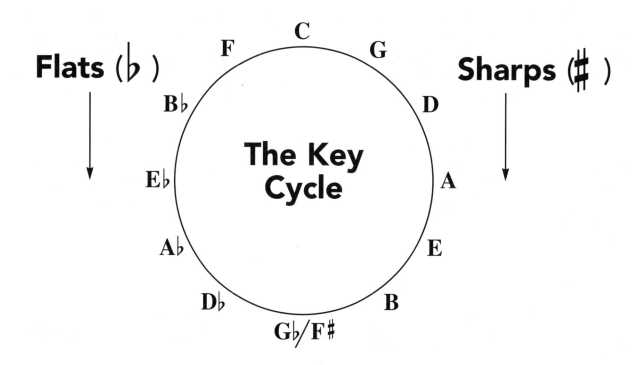

Think of the key cycle like a clock. Just as there are 12 points on the clock, there are also 12 keys. **C** is at the top and it contains no sharps or flats. Moving around clockwise you will find the next key is **G**, which contains one sharp (**F♯**). The next key is **D**, which contains two sharps (**F♯** and **C♯**). Progressing further through the sharp keys each key contains an extra sharp, with the new sharp being the 7th note of the new key, the other sharps being any which were contained in the previous key. Therefore the key of **A** would automatically contain **F♯** and **C♯** which were in the key of **D**, plus **G♯** which is the 7th note of the A major scale. As you progress around the cycle, each key introduces a new sharp. When you get to **F♯** (at 6 o'clock), the new sharp is called **E♯** which is enharmonically the same as **F**. Remember that **enharmonic** means two different ways of writing the same note. Another example of enharmonic spelling would be **F♯** and **G♭**. This means that **G♭** could become the name of the key of **F♯**. The key of **F♯** contains six sharps, while the key of **G♭** contains six flats.

If you start at **C** again at the top of the cycle and go anti-clockwise you will progress through the flat keys. The key of **F** contains one flat (**B♭**), which then becomes the name of the next key around the cycle. In flat keys, the new flat is always the 4th degree of the new key. Continuing around the cycle, the key of **B♭** contains two flats (**B♭** and **E♭**) and so on.